Renee? Todd -

Keep going - Beyond.

Emilee Mae

Start Here

THE RAW AND HONEST JOURNEY OF A NOMAD IN HER TWENTIES

Emilee Mae Struss

RIVER PLACE PRESS

START HERE

ISBN: 978-1-7376308-6-9 Print
ISBN: 978-1-7376308-7-6 eBook

Published by

40274 Diamond Lake Street
Aitkin, MN 56431
riverplacepress.com
chip@riverplace-mn.com
218.851.4843

RiverPlace Press is distinctive in guiding authors
through the maze of specialized publishing options,
with very personalized service.

emileemae.com

Published in collaboration with the Five Wings Arts Council.

FIVE WINGS
ARTS COUNCIL

For anyone still healing

Note to Readers

I find it quite funny, or no, perhaps ironic is the correct term to use here, that teenagers are supposed to know what they want to do with their lives—at eighteen years old. Thankfully, I was terrible with numbers, the most painfully extroverted introvert there ever was, and a frequent visitor of worlds imagined. I knew the only profession for me was to be a writer. A bleeding-heart, closet-liberal writer, who lives in northern Minnesota, feels things too intensely and cannot seem to settle down about it all.

That was me until I fell seventy feet out of a tree. Well, that's still me, but the falling out of a tree thing did change my life, as I'm sure one can imagine.

Some may say it's stranger than fiction, falling seventy feet out of a tree, and I'd have to agree. Even when I review this story, I grab my ribs and wince in pain. I get consumed by processing all the injuries and remembering how they felt. Painful. It was excruciatingly painful. But I must say, the pages enclosed here will reveal that while falling seventy feet out of a tree causes unimaginable physical pain, it cannot and never will compare to the pain that follows in the wake of heartbreak and loss.

The Velcro-separation of two souls, whose time has come to a close, leaves nerve-endings exposed. And the hole, like a cutout of one's center, when we lose the individuals we thought we could never live without, cuts deep into the sinews of one's most tender center where it bleeds.

And bleeds. And bleeds.

But I'm getting ahead of myself here. This story is about a young woman's search for meaning in life because it must be more than college. It must be more than partying and sleeping with guys you'll likely never speak to again. It just must be more than that, or that's what I wanted to discover by boarding a plane to South Africa on my twenty-first birthday and choosing to abstain from a single drop of alcohol. It was the greatest rebellion I could offer society at that time.

These years are the ones that made me who I am today. I hold them so delicately and with such reverence for their meaning in my life because before making me, they shattered every single part of me—to create something entirely new.

Thank you for reading my words; may they give you the space to speak whatever truth is most authentic to you.

START HERE

Life must be more than this, I thought. It was my third semester in college at Minnesota State University, Mankato (MNSU), and I was soon to be twenty-one years old. The day of my twenty-first birthday, February 5, 2014, I boarded a plane—to South Africa.

And I wrote a blog post.

It was titled "Giving 21 Its Dignity Back."

It went like this...

"Turning twenty-one usually means that the golden doors of legal alcohol consumption have finally swung open and access has been granted. Twenty-one has gained a reputation of uncoordinated footing, slurred words, and shameful actions.

Twenty-one never wanted this to be its reputation, but it is.

It's a time for experienced drinkers to hit the bars—and actually stay there past ten o'clock without getting kicked out. It's also a time for those that have waited patiently for the 'legal green light' to finally indulge. This makes twenty-one very sad. Twenty-one has another side to its personality, but few pay attention to it. It's a beautiful age of adulthood, independence, and responsibility. Twenty-one is still young, very young. Twenty-one is also *grown-up* and lightly aged by the two decades previous. Twenty-one has changed and learned from its actions. Twenty-one has dignity. Or, at least, I hope to give twenty-one its dignity back when we meet."

That blog post received the most views, shares, and comments out of any of my other blog posts. Mind you, my readership probably included my mother, my mother's friend, my best friend, and maybe one random visitor.

To get over 500 views on emmylou002.blogspot was a big deal.

It told me there was something here worth exploring—that maybe other twenty-somethings felt the same way? Maybe people of all ages, at times, feel this way? That there should be *more to life*. If we are truly the author, the architect behind our broken masterpieces, and the sole bus driver leading towards our souls' destiny, doesn't that mean we can craft our lives and stories however we desire? I mean *really* however we desire, without boxes to fit into or societal pressures to conform to or familial expectations to uphold—doesn't this mean we actually have the freedom to *decide*?

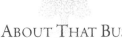

ABOUT THAT BUS

If you were a vehicle, what type of vehicle would you be? I like to think I'd be a boho camper van with succulent plants, an Aztec style décor, and a hardwood kitchen floor. That's definitely not what I was. In my early twenties, I was more similar to a yellow moped: single, bright with life, and on a mission.

That mission was to discover: *life must be more than this.*

But I was in college. College was this elusive thing that I'd heard people my parents' age speak of as "the best years of their lives." They sat around campfires and told stories, reminiscing of the good ol' times of college. Probably doing things they would not condone their children to do.

Just live it up! Is that what I was supposed to do? *We* were supposed to do? Just throw caution to the wind and splash around with underage drinking, sexual experimentation, and grades that barely pass as being present? I stutter-stepped my way from freshman to sophomore year, seeking a deeper meaning to life. I found a church to attend, called New Life Church. On a Monday, I attended five a.m. prayer meetings. By Wednesday, I believed it was all a hoax.

College life felt empty. The life, I mean "THE LIFE" just didn't feel like "THE LIFE." It felt like a waste of my time. And an extremely expensive waste of time. I felt lonely. Even though attending a large university meant that there were people my age everywhere, I still felt alone. Hundreds of students piled into auditoriums for classes and most of them didn't even make eye contact with another human the entire time. We all walked in, chose the same seat as we did the day before, pretended to listen, and then got up and walked out without speaking to another human.

I attended college, just three hours south of my hometown, a semester late due to a tragic climbing accident—I fell seventy feet out of a white pine tree in northern Minnesota. Yes, it's an absolute miracle that I'm alive, but more on that later. The point here is that I arrived feeling like I was given a second chance at life. I felt invigorated with the joy of life. And the students on that campus were just *killin' my vibe.*

Freshman year brought with it my first dark kiss of depression. This seemingly inescapable cloud that was not only dark, but could talk. It would tell me things like *you'll be alone forever* and *nobody will ever understand you.* Depression was also flashy with its lure of self-pity. It sucked me in and made me feel like I belonged there. The walls were black, the carpet was black, the door to enter into the state of depression was black—but at least I was welcome somewhere. At least I had a space to go. Something that could press on the rounded edges of my soft heart and make it feel something, instead of feeling numb. I had a roommate named Breanna. She barely left our small dorm room. Breanna had translucent white skin as if she truly had never seen the sun. She sat on her computer and watched YouTube videos for most of the day.

Meanwhile, I watched my friends on social media become Insta-besties with their new college friends. I felt like maybe if I had started college with everyone else, I could have done all those "Freshmen Week" fun activities and met new people. My "Freshmen Week" involved carrying my plastic shower tote to the girls' shower room and crying. It became a daily thing. I would go stand in the shower wearing foam flip-flops from Dollar General because people said freshmen get foot fungus if they stand barefooted in there, and I'd cry.

"It will get better, Em", my brother, TJ, said. At the time, TJ was a sophomore at the University of Minnesota, Duluth. He was really sociable, a natural track star, and therefore had many friends. It seemed like he was living up to the stories I'd heard my parents and their friends reminisce about. TJ also entered college with a few buddies from high school. I started telling myself that it would get better, and there was a group of friends forming on campus somewhere. My group of friends. They just hadn't found me yet, but thank God they were forming somewhere!

It wasn't true. There was no group of friends forming like I had in high school. I did, however, find a group of friends similar to myself with

MNSU's addition of a rock-climbing wall.

During my sophomore year, MNSU built an indoor rock-climbing gym that covered a corner wall space on the indoor track arena. It was stunning. At the rock-climbing wall is where I finally met my people. They were misfits, too. They were creative types and engineers. They were introverts, mostly.

One by one, my crew formed. Truth be told, not just one crew formed but two.

The second "crew" was my New Life Church friends. New Life Church wasn't your typical church. The first night I went there, I experienced a prophetic word. I didn't even know what prophecies were, or that they could happen in the present day. I thought prophecies only happened in the Bible, with Biblical characters. Not me.

A girl named Della, who attended the same high school as me and was a year older, called me one night. Randomly. I didn't even have her number. She said she got it from my brother. Della asked if I wanted to attend an evening church service. Grasping for anything to hold on to resembling hope, I said yes. She showed up with a girl who had almond skin and long, thick, dark hair. She wore a white tank top and hoop earrings. "Thuy" pronounced "Twee" was her name.

"What's good, boo?"

That's what she said to me.

The car was rattling with rap music. They were listening to Lecrae, a Christian rapper. I was surprised to hear that it was pretty good music.

We arrived at New Life Church, and a presence of peace welcomed me into this large cement building. We went in the back door like it was some secret meeting. Thuy and Della knew everyone. There was no rigid schedule or timeline. We didn't know how long we'd be there or what was going to happen.

"Let's lift our hands and just ask God what he wants to do tonight," said the pastor.

The pastor, I must confess, was young with caramel skin and very good-looking.

He carried on about the goodness of God, the presence of God, and then he said, "God wants to heal some people tonight."

He was pacing back and forth, and then he stopped and looked right at me.

Shit. I don't want to be "found out," I thought.

I wanted just to hide and observe.

He walked over to me, and Della began spewing bits of my story.

"Em's story is crazy! She fell out of this..."

He cut her off and said, "I just want to hear from the Lord right now."

I looked around the room as if the face of God might appear in one of the corners of the cement building. What would he look like, anyway? Or she? Male? Female? Genderless? The Bible says God is male, but the movie *The Shack* displays God as a Black female. I kind of liked *The Shack* version better, so I am very confused on this subject. Nothing manifested in physical form; however, there was me, this really good-looking pastor, and all these other young, eclectic people standing there with their eyes closed and hands lifted as if they were receiving something—a gift or a blanket—from God.

And then the visions came. He said, "I see a lot of physical healing, your body being woven back together," his eyes still closed yet standing a few feet from me. "I also see artwork, and God is using this artwork to heal you. I see your whole life, even your husband."

Umm, can I get a glimpse??

I broke down in tears. The things that he spoke of lined up perfectly with my story. The story of the tree. The miracle. The healing. Even the artwork, which was such a big part of my healing journey. Maybe this whole God thing really was real?

I Must Pause Here for a Moment

A moment of metaphorical silence, maybe, in honor of whatever "God" has looked like to you. I was raised Christian in a conservative family of strong Lutheran roots, who transplanted to the humble state of Minnesota. No sex before marriage, trust in Jesus, and life will be good. My journey since then has taken several footpaths away from this belief system. The word "God" is such a power word. It's a fight word and love word. It has caused wars and division among family members. It has also brought healing and breakthrough for many individuals. It has bound together broken family members and spurred restoration, even the impossible kind.

Without God, I must say, the things in this book wouldn't have happened. My God is a big God. He is a God of unconditional love. He is the God of second chances and then third, fourth, and fifth chances. He is the God of miracles. He is the God I call "He" because that's how I was raised when really, God is probably neither "He" nor "She." He is the God we want to see in order to believe. Especially in the Christian faith, because the Bible speaks of physical healing, and even when the healing doesn't come, and God doesn't manifest in front of us—we're supposed to keep believing.

Of course, it's perfectly natural for us to want proof of this almighty God's existence. To get the slightest taste of what could be God, we want gold dust to fall upon us, an angel to descend, a piece of paper to move, or a Bible to just fall off a shelf and flop open to Jesus' Sermon on the Mount, showing us that he is indeed the One True God. I was desperately hungry for more miracles because I'd just lived through an experience where only two percent are expected to survive. I understand this is due to many factors, including but not limited to: modern science, the speed of a helicopter, the medical professionals inside that helicopter, brave first responders, the hard-earned brilliance of doctors, my parents taking action, and the fact that my body was an eighteen-year-old person's body and not an eighty-year-old person's body (that would really be something).

But still, here I was, alive and with a shimmering, golden, living, breathing miracle on my record, as real as the day of my birth and the prints of my toes on my birth certificate.

Of course, I believed in God after that. What did I have to lose?

I believed that my God could heal. I believed that my God could reveal all that I needed. I believed that God could fill the void, the spot, the vacancy within me. I believed every single word that was ever written in the Bible.

In the same respect, there were moments where my big and almighty God seemed silent. As if God were holding the answers to my life above my head just out of reach like an annoying older sibling. I'd jump and cry and yell for Mom to come save me from this monster that's teasing me with something just out of my reach. Maybe Mom would show up, maybe she wouldn't. But even if she did, she can't remove me from my life's struggles. She can only support me through it, and tell me what she believes. It's up to us to make our own decisions.

Spirituality is something that must be experienced. One must choose to pack up their belongings and go on a quest for it, and, God forbid, they find answers that are different from the ones they were raised with. It might not even be the same religion or text. Perhaps not even from the same century hidden in history. But it is that individual's own path, discovered by them and nobody else.

Even though I've never found physical signs of God's existence, there is me. And this is what started my spiritual journey.

Back to the Story of Falling Seventy Feet Out of a Large White Pine Tree

Our camping tent could fit an entire circus inside of it, I'm sure of it. The green canvas structure came with large, heavy metal poles which took us *forever* to assemble. Forever, in an eighteen-year-old's mind, is about twenty-five minutes—just for reference. Setting the tent up was more of a team building exercise, because three different lengths of poles had to fit together just right to work. There was a lot of exchanging and questioning, but we finally did get our tent set up.

My father has always been an early riser. His ability to sneak out of the large canvas tent, with a six-foot-three stature, without waking my mother and I was truly something to baffle at. I woke to the smell of burning oak from the campfire. The sap bubbling and smacking from the fibers in the wood. Mom has never been an early riser. She laid like a zombie on the cot next to me.

I slid out of my military-grade sleeping bag and slipped into my sandals. Dad already had a pot of water boiling in a blue and white speckled tea kettle. Walking outside of the tent, I saw the oblong lake with cattails springing from the edges and two loons gently gliding along.

"Well, good morning!" Dad said as I tiptoed out of the tent.

I believe his excitement for seeing his children has remained the same since the first day he saw us enter this world.

When my mother woke up, I watched as she performed a very different type of coffee ritual. In the blue and white speckled tea kettle, she put coffee grounds... and an egg. As the egg cooked in the boiling water, it collected the coffee grounds and then boom—coffee. I was more astonished by this than the first time I saw a smartphone.

Our campsite was very remote because it was on a family friend's land. We camped there every summer. The unmistakable sound of an ATV motor in the distance grew louder as Kent, the landowner, paid us a morning visit.

"I brought life jackets, just in case you need some extra," Kent said. "If you go out in the canoes or whatnot, just make sure you're safe out there. I have a weird feeling this morning and just got nervous for some reason."

That same morning, my mother had a tense feeling in her stomach as well. She told Kent of the similar feelings she was having and reassured him that we would be safe.

We decided to test my ability to use a GPS and go for a hike. Our mission was to find this seventy-foot white pine tree that towered over the land. My dad had built a deer stand at the base of the tree. I found it more by following the dip of the land versus global positioning, but, nonetheless, I found the thing. And it was brilliant.

The prickled limbs were long and thick. I scaled the white ladder connecting the base of the tree to the first climbable limbs. I wrapped my hands around the limb and bits of bark rubbed off on my skin. The smell of pine grew stronger as I monkeyed limb after limb all the way to the top.

Peace. Pure peace is what I felt sitting there. I could see above the rest of the forest, and even the lake—which was about four miles away. I thought about God. *Is this what your spirit feels like?* I asked in faith. Just fresh air, the smell of pine, and an inner peace?

I was wearing jean shorts and a large red sweatshirt that read "Alaska" in cursive. It had thumb holes, not put there by the manufacturer, but by me, from wearing it too much.

"I'm coming down!" I yelled to my mother and father below.

The branch out in front of me was perfectly arched to grab with both hands. I did as I knew I was not supposed to and weighted the branch with all of me. Without a moment to react, the branch snapped.

My mind froze. I scanned quickly for anything to hold on to. I let go of the dead branch and entered complete shock. *I am going to die.* Not only am I going to die, but my parents will be the first ones to see my lifeless, dead body at the base of this tree. When I realized these were my abrupt last moments on earth, my mind actually removed itself from reality.

Sounds weird, let me explain:

The pain of smacking limb after limb, so hard that it broke six ribs, ripped my leg from its socket, and cut through the tender edges of my lungs—subsided to reach me. Like a low hum that grows loud and unbearable until all at once the sound just stops. Silence. My brain went silent, black, and distant.

An image appeared. It was me. Tubing behind a boat. I was getting whipped back and forth over the waves so fast I felt a well of fear in my stomach. I let go and smacked the water again, and again, and again. Normally, in real life, and not in some alternate dream reality to escape pain, the smacking would have stopped by now. But the blows kept hitting, sucking the oxygen from within.

It went on so long that my brain gave up on the idea altogether. And then I was in a dark alley with graffiti on the walls. Three men hovered over me kicking my ribs time and time again. There was no sound. No words. Just the idea of the action.

And then it all paused. The sun-sprinkled bluebird sky flooded my eyes and dusted away the blackness. Fuzzy lines of light contrasted with the tree limbs above me, and I heard something for the first time—my mother. Praying.

Her prayer was the confident words, "You were knit in my womb and you will be healed from head to toe."

Which, as I reflect on this, I realize sounds like the New King James Version of the story, but the words actually flowed out of her just like that. Exactly in verse form.

Now, while I was in my "alternate reality" of tubing and dark alleyway gangbanging, there were other sounds. Sounds I just couldn't hear: like my father's cries in the dense forest saying my name over and over again, my mother telling my father to call 911, and my lifeless body smacking tree limb after tree limb.

One hundred and twenty-two miles away, a Life-Flight helicopter rose from Robbinsdale, Minnesota, to meet an ambulance. In the air, the pilot communicated to the ambulance driver.

"We have a victim who fell seventy feet from a tree near Motley," the ambulance driver said.

"Seven feet? Copy."

"No, seven-zero feet, copy."

"So, we're picking up a body," said the pilot.

The forest floor was too dense to drive a four-wheeler in. Two first responders, one who happened to live next door, decided to drop the four-wheeler and hike into the woods with a stretcher.

Fading in and out of consciousness, I heard my mother yell, "Over here!"

The first responders arrived on scene and strapped me on the stretcher. My leg laid off the side, dangling by skin and detached by bone. The first responders tried to keep the stretcher straight to reduce the pain, but also get out of there as fast as possible. They kept telling me to stay awake. When I opened my eyes, there was a bright white light in the center of my view and the edges were fuzzy. I couldn't see the first responders; they were just pixelated bits of color. It was like using the aesthetic photography term "bokeh" in real life. Bokeh is defined as "the way the lens renders out-of-focus points." That's exactly what my eyes were doing. In this state, I could feel all of the pain. But I discovered a way to lessen the pain. It was to allow the blackness to begin at the edges of my eyesight, and slowly overwhelm the white light. As the blackness moved in towards the center, my pain lessened. Just as I was seeing almost complete blackness, and no pain, the first responders would snap their fingers and say, "Emilee, we need you to stay awake."

The blackness would recede, the blurred image reappeared—and so did all of the pain. I vacillated between the two, light with pain and dark without pain, for the entire hike out. I wanted to let go, and be released from all of it. We made it out of the forest and I was loaded into a small helicopter. There was little hope in my mind that I could handle the pain for another thirty seconds, let alone how long it would take me to arrive wherever I was going.

In the helicopter, I said, "I know you have something to knock me out. Please, give me anything."

She said she couldn't give me anything yet.

Slipping further and further into blackness, I don't remember the rest of the helicopter ride or landing at the Trauma Center in Robbinsdale.

In a white room, with people wearing white, I was shocked awake at the pain of a knife slitting my side and separating ligaments to reach my lungs. I screamed and writhed in pain. And then one last moment of silence. Finally, it all went black.

You Think It's Over and Then It's Not Over

When I woke up, there were tubes in my veins, my chest, over my face, and up my pee hole (or *pee-pee*, there's no delicate way of saying that one). I was swollen, queasy, and disrupted from reality with a wild dose of morphine.

But I was alive. *Holy shit*, I was alive.

TJ was the first person at my hospital bedside after the accident.

He recalls that I was awake and talking. No idea what I said to him, but he was able to console my parents, while driving two hours to the hospital, and reassure them that I was alive.

The next six days came and went without a beginning or an end.

They were strung together like a misty fog that hovers in space and moves in a spiritual stream. I remember snapshots of nurses coming in to change the tube bags. Bland cafeteria food appearing and then disappearing. My mom sitting. My dad standing. My parents welcoming friends and family. People talking to me, but I couldn't really understand what they were saying. Flowers and cards gathered in the windowsill.

One time I woke up to a circle of people standing around my hospital bed. Praying. They were all holding hands. Some of those people didn't even believe in God, but maybe they did just for this moment.

A sweet blonde nurse was replaced by a small feisty Asian nurse who told me I don't have an option whether I wanted to eat or not.

"You must eat food," she said.

The medications made me feel so queasy I didn't want to eat at all, but she was adamant. My mother began sneaking food into her purse to make it look like I had eaten something. I really didn't want to throw up with a chest tube in my ribs.

A middle-aged important looking man walked in wearing a white coat. He sat down with my parents and said that he had some X-rays to show us.

The first X-rays showed my pelvis and sacrum with fractured bones. Then my mid-to-lower spine with the small bones jutting off the vertebrae called transverse processes, all of which were fractured. Six broken ribs. A display of one completely failed lung, which appeared to have been photoshopped out from underneath my rib cage. The other lung was clearly smaller than normal.

"Her hip was out of its socket for about two hours," he said. "And it was an anterior dislocation, which is actually better than the opposite."

If the hip would have sat dislocated without blood flow to the socket for much longer, the entire socket would have died.

"She is an absolute miracle," he said. "She requires no surgeries."

My mother clapped her hands and put both of her fists up in the air like we had won a championship game. My father also clapped his hands. I was still out of it.

His next comment, however, made me snap back to life real quick.

"Was Emilee an athlete or active at all?" he asked.

"Yes, she is a runner and a triathlete," my father said.

"Unfortunately, her injuries are so great that she likely will never be able to run again."

While everything else through my blurred mind was fuzzy, those words and his facial expression was the clearest image I had seen yet. *"She likely will never be able to run again."*

I could no longer run. Could I walk? Would I be in a wheelchair?

Dad looked accepting but heart-broken. My mother locked eyes with the doctor and said, "She will run again."

Spit-fire of a woman she is.

To prove her faith on this subject, she took a pair of my brand-new orange running shoes and placed them in the windowsill.

Two days later, the blonde nurse returned to remove my chest tube. My mother helped me take a sponge bath for the first time since the accident. There were still clumps of pine needles in my hair. Two people dressed in street clothes rolled a wheelchair into the room and told me we were going to testing.

Still disoriented from the morphine, it was as if life was being played out in front of my eyes. The elevator door closed and we went down many floors. It opened to a dimly lit brick hallway. They rolled me into a room with a teacher-looking lady and a couple worksheets sitting on a table with two pencils.

"This is just to determine where your cognitive level is at," she said.

The street clothes clan rolled me up to the table, and I looked down at the worksheets that literally had drawings of playgrounds, apples, rulers, and happy faces around the frame of the worksheet. It was simple math.

I remember thinking, *it doesn't matter if I fell seventy feet out of a tree or not, I've never been good at this subject.* And I was all strung out on pain meds, so I started giggling at the little people smiling at me on the worksheet.

And then there was an extreme moment of realization and scenes from Adam Sandler's *Billy Madison* flashed through my mind.

I'm going to have to relearn *everything.*

Will they just put me up in the kindergarten class and I'll part my hair in pigtails again and relearn my ABC's with all the five-year-olds?

I had no measurement for how cognitive I was. Or wasn't.

They rolled me back upstairs and the man in the white coat returned. This was my final note of discharge.

My parents rolled me outside of the hospital. Sitting in the wheelchair, with my regular street clothes on and my limbs still swollen. My side was strapped with bandages from getting cut up by the tree. A three-inch-long hole sat just below my right armpit, still open and draining fluids from the tube placement. We walked underneath the awning and sunlight showered my skin for the first time since I had fallen. Healing. The sun felt like the grace of healing and a touch of comfort landing gently on my face like a butterfly. There was a park across the street with little water spouts popping out of the ground from colorful vents. Two kids ran in and out of the water, laughing and splashing.

The World Was Still Moving, and I Was Still in It

What did that even mean for an eighteen-year-old? I was stuck mainly on the doctor's firm words that I wouldn't be able to run again. Running was my freedom and joy. Light-footed and happy in heart, it was a big part of my life. Cut out? I couldn't imagine that, but I also didn't think I would survive falling seventy feet out of a tree. I began to question the true power of God. Instead of being angry at God, I wondered, what if I just cash all my chips in and trust that God would heal me? Completely?

God's spirit, during these intensely tender days of healing, were like tiny warm vibrations. I could feel them wrapping around my ribs and restoring them individually. Back in my hometown, my parents rearranged their living room to make it my bedroom because I couldn't walk upstairs. I didn't really know the meaning of the word "wince" until this experience. Each day, as night turned to morning, I would do several deep breaths and then press my chest up to a seated position. The shattered parts of my ribs shifted, and I winced in pain. The pain became a reminder that full healing was possible. I sat outside on the porch at my parents' house, which overlooks the Mississippi River. The river flows calmly, thin, and humble just miles away from its source. The next three months in 2011, slowly transitioned from sultry August days to chilly October mornings. I watched the trees transform from evergreen to muted gold, auburn, and scarlet.

The small bits of transformation that took place was symbolic in nature of my own healing. People came to visit me. Some of them I remember, others I don't. Reality was now one step away from the understanding of physical life. It was as if the taste of death, both bitter and sweet, pushed me beyond the physical realm. And even though I was alive and healing—my mind was still somewhere else. Somewhere pleasant. All the subtleties of life just weren't as heavy anymore. I pondered the growth of trees, the river's release, and how the seasons' transformations are small in a day and the opposite in six months. I smiled, relishing in the simplicity of daily life and the miracle of one breath.

LET'S JUST SAY, HYPOTHETICALLY, YOU DIED

You took your last breath. It's over. And then, wait, you came back. Yes, that's you—your lifeless body lying there, and then all of a sudden, your chest rises. Your lungs fill with air. Your eyes flicker open, and you see the sky with all the clouds. With a second chance at life, would you change things?

That answer for me was absolutely, yes. What matters now? The breadth of one single human life. I wasn't quite sure how to take that expansive playlist and break it down into digestible sound bites, but I held a greater capacity for the meaning of life.

I had all of this vigor for life, but what would I do with it? *Join the Peace Corps.* That's what I'll do! They travel to remote countries and do amazing work—that sounds like something meaningful. I'll do that. I researched Thailand, Sweden, Brazil, and Scotland. Totally random places. There was nothing calling me in any certain direction, the only thing I was certain of was that I needed to go *somewhere.*

While searching for a greater purpose in life, I believed that God was going to heal my body completely. I would be able to run again. The first steps I took were in the ladies' restroom in the mall. I crutched to the sink to wash my hands and then looked at the paper towels. They were (oddly) anchored to the wall next to the door. My mother and I looked at each other, and she said, "Are you going to do it?" I said yes and then took my first two steps to grab the hand towels and dry my hands. We clapped and cheered, in the ladies' restroom.

One year later, I signed up for a marathon.

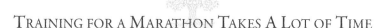

Training for a Marathon Takes A Lot of Time

Training for a marathon is one of the most time-consuming, arduous tasks ever. I moved out of the college dorms that summer and into a house with two other girls, devoting the summer to training for this marathon. The fifteen to twenty-miler days consumed all of my Saturday and Sunday mornings. During my runs, I would talk with God. I spoke with God about my life, my family, and my relationships. It grew into a sort of communion.

I had finally filled the hole in my heart. It felt like, truly, wherever I was—God was with me and his presence so tangible. It was as if we were two friends, continually chatting. During one of my long runs in late November, a guy wearing full-on gray sweats like Rocky Balboa, hood up, super-sexy scruffy face, and brown eyes, ran up next to me.

He said, "Where you running to?"

I said, "I don't know... I just run and choose my route along the way."

"Can I join you?"

Now, my Person (Emilee, that's me) begins talking to myself, saying this guy is maybe two years older and super-hot. Maybe we will fall in love, *so this is how it all happened*, I began imagining us telling people years later, *I was running when he saw me and we struck up great conversation and just never stopped being together after that.*

That's not how this went. Since before Rocky Balboa popped up out of nowhere, I was talking with God—that was still happening after he popped up, and the unsettling feeling in my stomach wasn't butterflies.

"Sure, you can join me," I said.

We start running along, and he tells me that I'm attractive, making a few comments about my ass (which, I have to say, is like the *worst thing* a guy can lead with). He called it that, "my ass," which is also an unattractive term, I think, but that's neither here nor there. We were here, on this paved sidewalk in the chilly fall air.

I started getting a little uncomfortable and ran faster. Soon, I could tell that his cardiovascular health wasn't as strong as the muscles bulging from underneath his gray hooded sweatshirt. And then, God led me down a different path. An assertive one. Which, isn't typically my style of personality.

"Do you think women like it when you talk to us like this?" I said.

"Like what?"

"Well, I don't know you, and I was open to running with you, and maybe getting to know you, but making comments like that is really not cool with me."

"I thought you would like it," he said.

I nodded my head, saying it makes sense, but no, I don't like it.

And then, this next sentence really came not from me: "*Do you use women often?*"

I thought, why did I just say that? Am I trying to get myself *killed*?

He stopped running and turned to look at me. I stopped running. We stood there on the sidewalk, just staring at each other.

I continued, "Does having sex with someone you barely know make you feel better about yourself? Honestly?"

"At the moment, I guess," he said. "But then, I don't know, I feel bad the next day or sometimes even right after because I know I have zero intentions of actually dating this person."

"Exactly," I said.

He really opened up after that, sharing that he doesn't know how to change his life, and he feels empty. I told him that, of course, he is empty. He is seeking things in life that have no purpose or meaning. I told him that I believe we all have a purpose in this world. He asked how to get "it."

"Purpose?" I asked.

"Yes, what do I do to not feel so empty all the time?"

"Pray," I said. "That's what I do I guess; I just trust that God or whatever spirit that needs to hear me will hear me."

After that, we stood there on the sidewalk and prayed together. He took off his knitted gray gloves (is gray the only color he owns?) and we prayed for him, for life, for choices, for making better choices, and maybe stop telling women they have nice asses—there are better word choices or compliments to make.

Before we went our separate ways, he asked for my name.

"Emilee," I said with a smile. "What's yours?"

"Israel," he said.

I never saw Israel again, but I did continue to pray for him. I was grateful that he was so open and vulnerable with a random girl he met on a sidewalk. My faith, at that point, was bulletproof. I believed that faith was all one needed to make the impossible possible. *It's what the Bible says!* Faith is all we need. If I wanted to walk on water, I bet I could—I'd trust Jesus to tell the stormy seas before me to "be still," and they would all stop, and he would go back to taking a nap in the boat while I carried on with my life.

In October of 2012, during my sophomore year, I laced up my running shoes to run a marathon. My body felt strong, my mind strong, and the words that "she'll never be able to run again," were so small. They didn't matter anymore because I was here, at the start line. The route was all tar. Looking back, I'd recommend running a marathon that is trail, and not all tar.

My feet felt light, thankfully, so I didn't feel like I was "pounding the tar," but it does add a little extra beating to the body. The day was cool, and the sun still warm. Marathons, I was told, should be run at "conversation pace." If you're doggin' out of breath, you're running too fast. My friend, Megan, had run a marathon prior to myself. She was the original inspiration when she casually asked me to run fifteen miles on a Saturday.

"Fifteen miles?" I said, shocked.

"Yeah, you run it slow. It's not so bad," she said.

I didn't join her that morning, but she made me think about what was possible. The Mankato Marathon was a great milestone for me—I had broken the curse that was no more running. Or so, I thought, at that time. I was still on my mission, like a true crusader for Christ, to travel around the world and share my unwavering faith. My mission came to me with a group of young people at New Life Church in Mankato— we were headed to Peru.

ARE GANG MEMBERS STILL DANGEROUS IF THEY'RE COMMITTED TO KNOWING JESUS?

Real question here while I was on my first overseas mission to Peru the summer of 2013. Jesus can change people, but when I was paired with an ex-gang member who used to carry a blade in his mouth for quick shank-access, I was a little nervous. We were in pairs for street ministry: one American, one Peruvian. The city we were in, Iquitos, is the largest city in the world that you can't drive to. Half a million people live in this Amazonian jungle, with a large percentage in extreme poverty. My group consisted of twelve, young, Jesus-loving, radical Christians. We didn't just randomly choose Iquitos. We traveled there to serve alongside a mission base started by a couple who used to attend New Life Church in Mankato. They moved there some years ago and started this men's ministry for recovering addicts. When we arrived, the mission base leader, Tito, gave us the following introduction:

"Our hearts are for this region. What that looks like is service. We have a men's safe house down the road, and we also accept those in recovery into our home. A prostitute with three children helps make meals. Our cooks are in recovery from addiction. We give the space for

Peruvians to meet Jesus, receive healing, and then give them a purpose within our home."

He looked tired. And I was tired from traveling on several planes (diminishing in size and safety as we progressed) to a bus that finally arrived at the mission base. Tito truly looked like a jungle man, and his children were little jungle children. They bathed in the Amazon River (Umm, hello! Aren't there like *piranhas* in there?). He had visually tough skin, short scraggly hair, and eyes that, if they could speak, would say, *won't you just give up and realize how much you're loved? Stop fighting.*

The mission base had a large open church with cement seating and two white stucco-walled buildings consisting of the mission couple's home and the guest house. There were no screens on the windows, not even glass. Everything was open. At the entrance of the guest house was an avocado tree. The limbs of the avocado tree drooped almost to the ground, full of fresh fruit.

A young couple from Texas lived on the base, caring full-time for an orphan they named "Quintin." Abandoned on the streets of Iquitos, they took the child in as their own and cared for him. Another child, who couldn't speak and had visible disabilities, was brought to the mission base by Tito—when he found the child being lured by several men to come with them. Tito believed the men would force the child into slavery, and therefore brought him to his home and named him "Amazon." He didn't speak much, and they called him "AZ"

AZ was extremely thin and easily amused. One could take an avocado off the tree and make a sound like "kerplunk" while the branch snapped back, and he would laugh for a longer-than-normal period of time. Joy. The little guy had complete joy. But he was also quite confused, and not sure about boundaries. As women, we had to create boundaries with little AZ, because he would get quite touchy in the chest region. It would start as a hug, and then wandering hands would just float to these round lumps that we have that he doesn't see on himself. AZ learned to have some boundaries while we were there.

We worked alongside the Peruvians for many things during our three-week visit. One of the most challenging was helping them build a new church. Sweating in the roasting sun, day after day, we followed their lead, hauling boards and bricks. The Peruvian men worked twice as hard as us. They were faster and hyper-focused on building a church for their community—a safe place. Outside of the church, the village was rotten with trash and disorder. Stray dogs scoured the streets. Their ribs countable, and their skin patchy with diseases. The shacks that lie alongside the road were creations of whatever materials they could find—cardboard, scrap metal, and discarded plastic. The entire village wreaked of sewage.

In the evening, those same men would meet in the large cement church on the base. They poured out their hearts during worship—with eyes drenched in tears. A previous drug dealer wore a bandana that said "Rey de Reyes," which means "King of Kings."

I tried to remain focused on worship myself, but I wanted to watch them. I wondered what it must feel like to receive grace after so much had gone wrong. These men, most of them had families. They had lost their jobs, marriages, kids or just lost direction in life. At twenty years old, I hadn't experienced such intense adversity in my own life. I didn't know what it would feel like to be so desperate for hope and experiencing life-crushing circumstances.

If someone were to ask me, "What's the worst thing you've done?"

At that point in my life, I would say, "Vote for myself to be homecoming queen."

Super-not-so-quick word on homecoming court—can we just not do that anymore to our young, developing, very fragile saplings which are so insecure about themselves and just want to be liked by everybody?? Literally *everybody*. I don't have an offering for an alternative, but it puts like twelve people on a pedestal out of 700. I was one of those twelve people and was shocked when they called my name over the intercom system, and then I got a million texts on my flip phone saying, *"Congratulations, you made it!"* and *"I knew you'd make it!"* I felt excited and also guilty. What if my one vote for myself upset the entire bracket??? I am a fraud, that's what I decided about myself—but I put a pretty dress on and smiled and waved anyway. So, there you have it—the truth about homecoming. I wish everyone could be on homecoming court, but that would defeat the purpose of it in the first place. Like I mentioned previously, I don't have an alternative to offer; I'm just saying that homecoming court is a lot of pressure. To make it! To keep it! To be perfect! Smile! Bright! Talk! Loud! LAUGH LOUDER. Be wanted.

Act like you don't need to be wanted. Walk with confidence. Do what boys tell you to do. Eat nothing. Ever. Why are you not dating anyone, btw?? He likes you!! Date him!

Dating in high school wasn't a trend that I subscribed to. I hadn't met many men I was truly interested in dating, so I felt—why would I waste my time? It wasn't until I met a man on a beach named Dominique that make me think otherwise. The part of the country I grew up in, however, didn't exactly promote interracial couples. I knew not one other interracial couple. Dominique was the quarterback for the community college, and I was still in high school. He introduced himself over a conversation with his teammate who had recently shaved his head completely bald. "Excuse me, miss," he began, as his friend next to him laughed and told him not to ask me about his bald head. "My friend here just shaved his head, and I think he took it a little too far this time," he said, smiling. "What do you think?"

I laughed at such an odd question and said it looked just fine.

"Yeah," his friend said to Dominique, "see, it's just you that thinks I'm too bald, man, lay off me." We walked to the parking lot laughing, and he asked for my phone number—saying he'd like to keep talking.

We talked daily for a few months, and I told my brother about him. I went to his games and he'd visit me on the sidelines in his sweaty pads and take his helmet off to reveal his thick braided hair pulled back by a rubber band. I liked him, and somehow, in northern Minnesota, I'd found someone like Dominique. And then, a news article was published sharing horrific news that I still, thirteen years later, am not sure how to process—he had been shot. When he was home visiting his mother, he was shot outside his mother's house in Indianapolis. He died soon after. My brother messaged me the article and said, "Is this the guy you've been talking to?" I said yes, and then I didn't date again until college—four years later. That was the first time I realized how far we had to go as a country for there to be race equality. I would never have been shot moving my mother's car outside of her home in Brainerd, Minnesota. However, twenty-year-old, smart, and very talented Dominique, was, in Indianapolis.

In Peru, I began to process my first understanding of what the word *privilege* meant. The fabric of my life, the sole fact that I was born and raised in the United States of America, put me in a completely different category. Not one that I worked to receive. Not one that I deserved. It just was. I was privileged to live in a nation that educated me. I was privileged to be raised in a family with a mother and a father who were still married. I was privileged to be white. I was privileged to have the chance to travel. To even be here with those hurting, to a depth I couldn't begin to understand, I was privileged.

During our second week in Iquitos, we took a straw boat to a remote village along the Amazon River. I was pretty sure that the boat was going to sink. The water's edge waved just underneath the tips of straw bound together and sticking up. The straw holding all of us.

The people living in the village had never been outside of the village. Their lives, from start to finish, all happened here in this remote area. They had a small school and a tiny hospital clinic. I mean, like one single room with faded info-graphs showing how to do CPR. Pretty sure the correct guide to CPR had changed about seven times already since that poster was hung.

We brought tents and slept in a "community building." It had a wooden floor and bound straw covering for a ceiling. I started to realize that maybe this straw is more reliable than I thought. The men in the village woke up at four a.m. to catch fresh fish from the river for us. The women boiled the fish, and we were to eat them whole. That was a new experience for me. I've eaten filleted fish from lakes, but never eaten a fish that was staring back at me before. Somewhere along the line, I contracted a nasty parasite in my stomach. I couldn't keep anything down and just kept throwing up in the dewy grass beside the wooden community building. Three women saw me throwing up and told me to come inside the building. They helped me roll out my sleeping bag and put a homemade mixture into my water bottle. The women told me that they were missionaries from Africa. They shook my water bottle with the mixture in it and said, "Drink this entire thing. We will be back in a few hours. You should have the entire thing down by then."

I thanked them and wondered if I had just experienced angels in real life. As I was sitting there, drinking this mixture, one of the pastors came running into the shelter. His face looked concerned, and he was yelling, "We need clean t-shirts!"

I wasn't sure why, but I just did as I was told and rummaged through my bag to find one.

In the village, there were many safety hazards. One of them was these long impale-potential posts. I think they were supposed to be part of a fence, maybe the beginning of a fence. Whatever they were, they turned out to be a great hazard. One of the village boys was climbing a tree (I could've told him that was a poor idea) when he fell out of the tree and onto one of these posts. Two of the women in our group were nurses and rushed to the scene. The boy's father went to pull the stick out. It went in near his hip, piercing his back, and came protruding out of his shoulder. The two women told the boy's father that the stick needs to remain in there. Otherwise, he would lose too much blood. With the t-shirts soaking up blood leaking beside the stick from his side, they took the boy back to the straw boat and slowly floated their way back to Iquitos. The boy went to a hospital in the city and slowly recovered. I wondered what would have happened if our team hadn't been there? Would the father have just pulled the stick out of the boy's back, and that would be the end?

It was a reality check for me once again. In my circumstance, I was *airlifted* to a hospital with some of the best doctors in the world. Somewhere in my heart, I felt guilty. And I felt jealous. It was odd. I felt guilty because I had access to all of these modern amenities. And even basic ones, like food, shelter, and healthcare. But I felt jealous because this boy's life was so simple. His life wasn't built upon an endless list of choices. As adolescents in America, we are told that we can do anything. I bet nobody ever told that little boy he would need sunglasses because his future is so bright. No, you get your hands dirty working in the village alongside your sisters and mamas. Me getting my hands dirty in America looked like trying to stay true to myself while being greatly swayed by what I thought I was *supposed* to want. Some people spend the bulk of their life living somebody else's dream—be it the dream their parents had for them or society had for them. Eventually, they reach an age where they think they were supposed to "have it all together by now," and they become depressed. Because they don't have it all together. They're in their mid-forties and still don't know what they want. Is this my dream? Is this my parents' dream for me? Is this my spouse's dream?

In America, we have to be brutally honest with ourselves. On a smaller scale, it's like the toothpaste aisle. This one always gets me. We have an entire aisle just for toothpaste options. There are shiny boxes with promising phrases that say things like "Whiter smile in just fifteen days!*." And then you have to go search for the "*disclaimer" because there's probably some stipulation on the back of the box that says, "not clinically proven." Then there are the natural-toned boxes that make me think it's natural ingredients. Do those toothpastes even work? There are big boxes, two-for-one boxes (better deal?), small boxes, and some toothpastes don't even come in a box.

Each of those toothpaste boxes is like a symbol of the choices we have in America. We do have endless choices, but make the right one. Don't mess it up. Don't do what your father or mother did. Don't do what your sister did. And dear GOD, don't do what your uncle did. Make the right decision. Be parts of all of those people, but still balance on the thin line that makes you, you.

After one week, our group returned to the mission base to begin jail ministry in Iquitos.

Another reality check. While my team members hopped in, praying and singing with people in jail, I rocked back and forth against a wall with extreme stomach pains. But I was there. I was present. And once again, I looked at these men and their situations and pondered God's grace. They were stuck in jail for who knows how long because of something they did or were involved in, and now they were just praising Jesus? It was a backward kind of experience. The jail was made of gray cement and no roof. The room where they hosted church was wide open to the skies above. Small puddles of water were dispersed on the floor from precipitation the day prior. There were two types of men I could see here: the ones with hope and the ones without hope. They were in the exact same place, with two different lives. They ate the same, slept the same, wore the same ratty clothes day after day—yet the ones in the church had joy. Some type of joy that, I felt, couldn't be taken away. Not even by life in jail.

What was that joy? What was that hope? And how could I harness it and bring it into my life? So *American* of me, to see something amazing and quickly desire it for myself. My life had no physical bars around it, only the ones in my mind. I was trapped inside myself. The only way out was to free my mind. These men were proof. It wasn't the circumstance that gave them happiness. Their circumstance often doles out quite the opposite. Instead of accepting the defeat of their past, they were here looking to the God of grace. The God of second chances. The God of healing.

I rocked back and forth, not only in pain for my sour stomach, but in compassion for these men. They were here—showing up to allow change. Even when the situation didn't look good, they were there—showing up. Changing what they still had the power to change.

I Was Set—I Wanted to Be a Full-Time Missionary

I didn't even know what being a full-time missionary meant, but it sounded like it included travel and taking care of people less fortunate than myself. I liked that idea—that was something I could do. It had a lot more meaning than college. But by this point, I had developed actual friendships. I liked my life. I read the book *Kisses from Katie*, an account of a young woman giving up her American life to live a life of service in Uganda. I held it close, and prayed for her story to be my life. In her book, Katie Davis recounts that she didn't necessarily want to give up her American life, but she felt led to.

One year after Peru during my junior year of college, I announced to my family that I was going overseas… somewhere. The "where" would be revealed in its own perfect timing. I cancelled all of my fall semester classes, moved out of my four-bedroom apartment I shared with three friends, and moved into a family friend's home. I told them I'd only be there for a month or so.

I prayed and prayed, *God lead me where I am supposed to go. Use me however you want. I don't want to live a mundane college life. Will you just provide a way for me to make a greater impact in the world?* Months went by, and I was beginning to make myself look crazy and God look like a fool. And then, all of a sudden, it changed. In a shoe store in Mankato, Minnesota, when I met a saleswoman named Tammy.

It started with these green Keen shoes I had bought for the mission trip to Peru. I didn't wear them once, so I went to the store to return them. Tammy, a short and very stout woman of about fifty years old, asked why I had bought them in the first place. I told her about Peru, and what I hoped to do next with my life.

Her eyes, the most piercing blue, lit up as she shared about a place in South Africa called Project Heal—a place she traveled to yearly, and was headed to again this upcoming February. I asked if we could meet to discuss it more. The next day, Tammy and I were sitting in a booth at Perkins, eating maple-syrup-soaked pancakes, and drinking coffee talking about Project Heal. Everything in me said "yes" to traveling with this woman. So, I asked if I could go with.

"Are you serious? That's only a few months away. You can't just leave college?"

"Yep. Already have."

Tammy wasn't so sure, but she prayed about it. Eventually, she told me that she too, felt it was right. I bought a ticket to stay in South Africa for three months. Tammy planned to stay for three weeks.

She got on her return flight. I, however, did not.

VERY LITTLE DO I REMEMBER ABOUT THE ACTUAL TRAVELING PART

It felt like a week on an airplane. Sleeping with makeshift blankets and on backpacks in international airports. Drinking bottled water. South Africa's time zone is seven hours ahead of U.S. Central Time. This made me wonder if I had truly just moved forward in space and upset the linear progression of life. Did I lose seven hours of life or gain it? This was too much for my tired brain to process. We arrived in the middle of the night, and my soon-to-be housemates picked me up. They showed me to my room, and I crashed out.

When I finally woke up, sweaty and well rested, it was the middle of the afternoon. I heard my housemates speaking with a woman downstairs. I realized it was Cindy, the Executive Director of Project Heal. I ran down the stairs and told her I could be ready to go in five minutes.

"Just take this day to rest," she said. "I will come back tomorrow."

I felt guilty for having slept well into the afternoon, but I was on the opposite side of the world now. My housemates, Analeigh and Jenco, were

Afrikaans (a-fruh-kaanz), of Dutch descent. Their language came off extremely passionate in everything that was spoken. I often mistook it as aggression, wondering if they were angry with one another. They spoke English to me, and oftentimes—Afrikaans to each other or visitors. Their house was a small two-story home. My bedroom was upstairs with two twin-sized beds in it. I laid my large zebra-print suitcase on one of the beds and sat on the other. I was actually here. In South Africa.

Analeigh and Jenco both had round faces with eyes of strength and light. Jenco had a large beard, one he would stroke while thinking or waiting. The couple attended the same church as Cindy, and they had volunteered to host me during my stay. I paid rent, and they took care of everything from driving me places to making meals. The meals—they were something. I discovered South African cuisine that I had never heard of before, like chutney. They used this thing called "chutney" on everything. It was like a fruit jam that was used as commonly as ketchup in America. It was delicious. And buttermilk rusks! Rusks are these double-baked, texturized stalks of buttermilk and grain. They look like biscotti, and are quite similar. Some evenings before dinner, Analeigh, Jenco, and I would have instant coffee with rusks. I think if I had those exact ingredients with me today but in an American context, it wouldn't taste the same. It was the experience that made afternoon instant coffee and buttermilk rusks taste so good. The layers sunk into and soaked up powdery coffee, making the cheap taste of the little dissolving particles leave the lingering feeling of happy memories.

South Africa was patchy. And by patchy, I mean some parts were really quiet and well-kept, other parts were in complete unrest. One might think *isn't that any country in the world*? But no, South Africa was like this just blocks apart. The division between cultures was palpable, not only to the eye but also in spirit. On one side of the road could be mansion homes with bronze gates and spikes on top. On the other side of the road could be thousands of people living in poverty. They don't speak the same language, or even share similar lifestyles—yet they shared the same road to get to their homes.

Analeigh and Jenco's house was on a plot of land owned by their church. The church was just up the road, and the pastor's house was a few houses away from theirs. Their little community was encircled by a gate. The windows on their home had metal, instead of screens. Little green lizards, and even deadly spiders, could climb through and scurry about on the walls. What, or who, I wondered, were they trying to keep out? Analeigh and Jenco were relaxed, and therefore, so was I, but the barred-up windows, although in a lovely antique design, made me wonder.

Cindy arrived the next day in a white "bucky," or a small pick-up truck. She had a topper on the back and picked up workers on her way to work. I wore a bright orange shirt, one I wore often while running, and sat next to a quiet young man in the back of the bucky. He was an after-school group leader. That afternoon hundreds of kids piled into the entrance of the humble Project Heal's entrance. Clearly, they each had their routines and their go-to areas. Two little girls hung upside-down from the monkey bars and spoke quickly in Xhosa. A moment on this language: Xhosa or "isiXhosa," as they call it, is a Bantu (sub-Saharan African people group) language with click consonants. Five-year-olds can make click sounds with their mouths that I cannot even attempt. One sound, native English speakers could attempt, is to air-tight seal your tongue to the roof of your mouth. As the pressure builds, smack the tip of your tongue off the roof of your mouth. That's just one of their eighteen click consonants. Clicks are part of the whole of a word. This language, I found wildly captivating. It was like their village's own secret language. I just wanted to know it, to speak it, and to understand it as they did so effortlessly.

Back to these kiddos. They knew where to go on the grounds of Project Heal, and it was clear they felt at home there. Seven boys ran to the soccer fields and began kicking the ball back and forth. Other kids circled up and sang songs and chants. It was the chaos of maybe one-hundred kids that day.

And they weren't all little. Teenagers came strolling in later, with their flip-phones playing Beyoncé songs on repeat. I was surprised by their apparel—all American. Their clothes were straight out of a GAP commercial. I didn't understand why they would choose to wear what Americans wear, when their culture has so many bright and lively prints they celebrate as traditional? So, I asked one of the group leaders named Kai.

"We all want to live the life that you get to live," he said. "We just want to be Americans."

"Why?"

"Because life is just better there, life isn't good here. It's hard here."

I gravitated to spending time with the teenagers that afternoon, interested in learning more about how they view their culture. One girl with thick braided hair that draped well below her waistline asked, "What's it like in America?"

"Is it just like in the movies with yellow taxis everywhere?" Asked another girl.

"No, I said, that's just in New York City, which, you've probably seen in movies," I said.

"Is it big? How far away are you from New York City?"

"I'm like twenty-three hours away, drive time," I said.

They were rocked by this fact, as all they'd seen on television was New York City, and so that must be where all Americans live—right there in busy Times Square.

They asked if I know Beyoncé, with big hopeful eyes. I had to tell them that, unfortunately, I do not know her in person.

The kids came from a village called Mzamomhle (mm-za-mum-shlay) in Eastern Cape, South Africa. Thousands of people living in shacks and ultimately—in poverty. The shacks, made of tin, cardboard, and other scrap metals, were packed so tight that you could barely walk between them. They cannot withstand strong winds or rainstorms.

I wanted to learn more about these teenagers. The next generation refused to wrap the banner of their country's past and thereby, culture, around their shoulders. They wanted to create something new, and it looked a whole lot like America. Their parents were quite proud to be from the Xhosa people group. They wore traditional wares with zig-zagged prints of bright contrasted colors and head wraps. Every Wednesday, Project Heal hosted an event called "Masikanye," it was an educational meeting for women.

WHITE PRIVILEGE

At this point, I grew even deeper in awareness of my own white privilege. Or, *American* privilege. The lessons that we were teaching to the mamas visiting Project Heal for Masikanye were simple—rights to their own bodies, rights to their own lives. They had rights that they were

1. Unaware of, and 2. Afraid to use. The culture here is best described by a man named Tom, the Project Heal custodian.

He stayed in one of the houses on the property. In the home with him was his wife, son, and grandson. Tom had a porous face and a humble heart. Every evening, when the kids left, Tom walked over to the main house to clean the dishes. He cleaned the house every night in a blue jumpsuit. One evening, I asked Tom about his story. He didn't know a lot of English, but he smiled a toothy (many of them missing) smile, and said, "My story?"

He was standing at the sink in the kitchen over a pile of hundreds of colored plastic plates. His hands full of soapy suds. Tom shook his head, looking down at the plates, and said, "You want to know *my* story?"

Then he laughed, like I was crazy. I started to laugh as well, more out of awkwardness than anything else. He took his hands out of the soapy water, and plated them together as if he were about to hand me over a physical story book.

"My story is this," he said, "I use to think woman less than me." His brown eyes were wide and eyebrows raised. "I tell wife, 'Do this for me and that for me...' and she very sweet lady and do all thing for me."

Tom began to shake his head, as if he were ashamed of that man.

"Then," he said, holding up a pointer finger, "I read word of God. Word of God say I must honor woman. I must love her as myself. I realize, I must change. I must honor wife, and I must do thing for her. You see— God change heart. That is what happen in my life. God change heart."

He put his hands on his heart, still wet with suds, and smiled. His eyes bright with light.

"Thank you for sharing that with me," I said. "God changes hearts."

"Yes! That's it. God change heart."

The village of Mzamomhle is a very unsafe place for women. Project Heal was there to change that. Their approach was to provide meals, education, and training for the youth—to project a more equal, and safe, future. They designed a safety system within the village for kids and women to go to if they were being abused. It was to put a certain colored cloth outside of their shacks. If someone needed a place to go—they could just look for this specific type of cloth. Each night, as the kids piled onto Project Heal grounds, I wondered about the pain of their lives. What had they experienced? It was a glimpse into this story that led

Cindy to quit her executive-level position with Mercedes-Benz and start a non-profit organization.

It started with two little African girls who walked miles to attend the same church as Cindy. She began to talk with them at church, and looked forward to seeing them every week. One Sunday, only one girl showed up. Cindy asked where the other little girl was, and she informed Cindy that her friend had been raped and killed. Burdened by this little girl's story, Cindy began to pray that God would provide a way for her to do something. Cindy looked at her own life and thought, while she was making very good money, she couldn't allow things like this to happen. She prayed, and prayed, and prayed. And then she made the decision: she was leaving her cushy job to start a nonprofit near this little girl's village. Mercedes-Benz, when they received the notification of Cindy's resignation and the reason behind it, bought the plot of land for her to begin Project Heal.

Cindy told me this story one evening while we sat at her kitchen table in her home. It was a two-bedroom home, all white and glowing, just a few blocks from the coastline. We shared a meal, and had peaches for dessert. At this point, Cindy had been running Project Heal for about ten years. I wanted to soak up every word from this woman, whose whole life was committed to bettering the lives of others. A single woman, who had escaped an abusive marriage years before. She said during our chat, "There were times when I thought I was going to have to sell my house because Project Heal wasn't making enough money."

God provides, is what she says. I got to see this, in real-life. One afternoon, the workers came to Cindy and said, "Mama Cindy, we don't have enough food to feed all of the kids coming here after school."

Cindy, it seemed to me, looked unmoved. She said, "Pray. God will provide."

That's what they did, and then two hours later, a man knocked on the front door of Project Heal. He said he had a truckload of food from the grocery store that he couldn't sell because of the expiration date. The workers hauled in load after load of food, just smiling away.

Project Heal was designed originally as an after-school program for youth. Education in the village is one of extremely low quality. Cindy believed that if she could help educate the youth, provide healthy meals, and teach them to treat each other as equals—it would change the future of Mzamomhle. The day-in and day-out seemed daunting to me. Cindy was always "on call." People broke into the buildings and stole things that were gifted to them such as computers and headsets. If a situation, such as abuse, were happening to one of her own in the village, she would drive right in there and get them. She wasn't afraid. That's what I noticed early on about Cindy—she wasn't afraid. And she shared with me that she thought I was fearless, as well.

"Most volunteers I have to encourage to 'get out' a little bit and not be so afraid of the streets," Cindy said. "But with you, I feel like I have to ratchet you back a bit and tell you to be safer."

I felt completely safe there, and ventured out each night for a five-mile run along the South African coastline. Waves crashing off the rocks released a salty dew into the air. I could taste the sea salt as I ran by the oceanic stretch. I began to attend a church in the village, where we met in a classroom with beaten-up desks, open windows, and a chalk board backdrop. The sermon was in Xhosa. I couldn't understand a single word—besides "mlungu." It means "white person." The pastor said this term once, and I knew he was speaking of me because I was the only white person in that entire room. I just smiled, and then he laughed—knowing that I understood that one word. It didn't matter that I couldn't understand the words. The feeling—the spirit—was the same.

This, I thought, was my higher calling. I was meant to be here. The thing I had been searching for back in America was right here with these kids. My three months went by slow in a day and fast in a week. With my time, I taught writing and reading in English and an art class. I took on more responsibility, the further my time went on. Maslow's hierarchy of needs began to look, to me, more like a circle than a pyramid. Maslow's five-stage pyramid originally created in 1943 says that humans must satisfy lower-level deficits before achieving higher-level ones. From the base of the pyramid moving upward, the needs are: physiological (basic needs like water and food), safety (security), love and belonging (friendship), esteem (accomplishment), and self-actualization (achieving one's full potential). According to Maslow, needs at the base of the pyramid must be satisfied before one can move to the higher-level needs such as esteem and self-actualization.

Being raised in a middle-class American family, I never once had to wonder where my next meal would come from. There was love, so much love, abounding in that house. I was cared for, and given the best opportunity possible for pursuing higher education and making a life for myself. But it was just that—a life for *myself*. It didn't seem fair to me that I could just skip on my merry white way to higher education, when so many didn't have access to it themselves. What could I do about it? These kids were stuck in the bottom tier of Maslow's hierarchy—either in physiological or safety needs. One afternoon, we did an exercise with the kids and wrote the following on a poster board: Food, Shelter, Safety, and Love. We asked the kids which one of these they desired the most. Their answer? Safety.

Above food. Above shelter. Above *love*. When I say Maslow's pyramid is a circle, is to point out here that I had all those things. I was not lacking in any area, but it wasn't fulfilling to me. America, my family, my socioeconomic class, and my ethnicity had given me all the rungs of the ladders to climb this pyramid with ease. Food and water? Get it from the fridge. Safety? Dad served in 'Nam, I'm good. Belongingness? My family is always there for me, supporting all my, at times, half-brained, ideas. Esteem? I competed athletically and performed well. I won awards. I was in college and doing well. Self-actualization? Here's where I wanted more. Where was the next ladder? Instead of climbing higher, the next move was to stick my feet back down every single one of those rungs until I sat face-to-face with the beautiful people at the base of the pyramid. I was given the greatest chance to just keep rising, but where's the fulfillment in that? How am I rising if I'm not taking others with me?

It was here, in this moment of understanding, that I decided to stand in line at home affairs for two days and extend my visa for four more months.

Home affairs was a terribly rundown place. It was a long line of me and a bunch of Zimbabweans. Why? Because Zimbabwe's economy had just collapsed. In 2009, Zimbabwe stopped printing their own currency because they had experienced "hyperinflation." Recounts were made of people walking to the grocery store with a wheelbarrow of cash to buy a loaf of bread. Their peak month of inflation is estimated at 79.6 billion percent between 2008 and 2009[*]. By 2015, they had completely stopped using their own currency all together, and adopted the U.S. dollar. And there was war. The year I was in South Africa, 2014, the Zimbabwean

---

[*] I found this statistic on Wikipedia. I know Wikipedia isn't the best source (I apologize to my high school English teacher), but it was a legit article about Zimbabwe's inflation titled "Hyperinflation in Zimbabwe."

Prime Minister made a declaration that all white Zimbabweans should "go back to England" and called for Black Zimbabweans not to lease any agricultural land to white Zimbabweans. Just like South Africa, there were both white and Black people from the same nation. White Zimbabweans were referred to as "White Rhodesians," and were of European descent. They aren't a big part of the population, only about six percent at its height, but they were heavily involved in farming and owned land. We heard stories of farms being destroyed, and White Rhodesians massacred in the process. Zimbabweans fled to South Africa to find jobs. The president of South Africa, Jacob Zuma, had another response to this: shut it down. Shut. It. All. Down. President Zuma didn't want immigrants fleeing into South Africa, so he put a ban on everyone looking to extend their stay in South Africa. When I finally made it to the upstairs room with one man sitting in it and stacks of papers on a table behind him, he stamped a piece of paper and gave it to me. I paid him. I thought I would be okay, I thought I'd pass.

With my new stamped passport, and 300 US dollars to change my flight, I had a new return date. I extended it by four months. And then immediately regretted it. I woke up early in the morning, like three a.m. early, sweating, thinking about life back in America. I was suddenly homesick and terrified that my grandmother, who wasn't very healthy, would pass. I walked to a small patch of woods in Analeigh and Jenco's backyard and sat there—feeling sick with anxiety. Rocking back and forth and praying that God bring me some stillness and peace. When Analeigh woke four hours later, I cried, clung to her like a child, and told her how I was feeling.

"This was your decision, and there is a reason you felt this way. It will be okay, just enjoy the extended time here," Analeigh said.

I did my best to release my anxiety. What would I do with an extra four months in Africa? I thought about the teenage girls that attended Project Heal, the ones who asked me if I knew Beyoncé. I asked myself, what were the most special times of my teenage years? Prom. I loved getting dressed up, and attending dances. So, I decided to plan a prom, with no real vision of how it would be accomplished.

With paper and pencil, I wrote out all of things necessary for an excellent prom:

Dresses—and not just any dress, *THE* dress
Hair and make-up
Photographer
Dance music with a good sound system
Legit DJ
Dance-floor
Delicious dinner with desserts
Elegant décor and flowers

It's a snapshot of time for every young girl to pause and release all of her insecurities. When I was sixteen, I wouldn't step foot into my high school if I didn't have make-up on, or if my hair wasn't straightened. It was the trend in 2009 to have straight hair—my hair is naturally wavy. There were many reasons I wrote myself off. I have freckles, and my stomach isn't perfectly flat, I didn't have the coolest clothes and there was a gaping all-consuming misconception that I was a cool kid.

Despite all of these insecurities, I found myself at the "cool table" during lunch with the "popular kids." I figured it was because my brother was the true "cool kid," and I was kind of just grandfathered in, if you will. I felt massively out of place. Truly, I felt most connected to the clique referred to as the "druggies." The kids that skipped out on most of school, except art class. They busted their asses to make it via skateboard from the gas station where they were bumming cigarettes from old men—back to art class. These kids had seemed to discover a pocket of the I-don't-give-a-fuck-its and they expressed that. I felt like I had to be a proper popular girl and say the right thing, hang out with the right boys, do well in school, and be admired. I should watch what I eat, and never ever do anything to embarrass myself or jeopardize my standing in the popular crowd.

The druggies didn't care about any of that. They wore black eyeliner and leather on their bodies in creative ways, and they had piercings in their noses and eyebrows; they seemed confident in themselves. My freshmen year of high school, I sat on my parents' porch and cried in fear of my senior year—that I wouldn't get asked to prom.

"Nobody likes me!" I said.

"Em, that's four years away still," my brother said. "Don't worry about it."

My mother added things like, "You're a stunningly beautiful girl" and "You have nothing to fear."

I didn't feel that way. I felt rejected and just a little too far off from the mark of what makes a young woman beautiful or desired.

My senior year came, and I never was asked to prom. *That* was my choice. I had attended dances before with dates, but this time—I wanted it to be sacred for me. I went with a group of friends, and it was the best dance of them all. I wasn't worried about anything expect for enjoying my time as a senior in high school. Our school did prom quite big, with a grand walk and everything. One of my guy friends asked me to walk with him, and we are still friends today. There was no expectation of me that night. Not to be promiscuous or to be in-the-know. Not to dance with a certain person or figure out where the best after-party would be. That night, it was special for the making of me.

With my list of items to make an excellent prom for these girls, I went to work calling potential donors. Besides planning the prom, I was still assisting with after-school classes for the kids, and at times, visiting an orphanage with Analeigh. This is where she met her first baby girl— Ada.

In poverty-stricken areas of South Africa, when mothers cannot care for their babies, they sometimes abandon them. Newborns have been abandoned in ditches, on the doorsteps of random people's homes, and even in public places. The orphanage that Analeigh and I visited had rescued newborns from all of these locations. About fourteen little ones, with severe diaper rash and an unending desperation for attention, crowded the small orphanage. Ada was three months old when we first met her. She was dressed in a white onesie with little pink pants that had ruffles at the feet. Every part of her was round—her little toes and fingers, her belly, her cheeks, and her dark brown eyes. It was a visceral reaction, within both Analeigh and me, of wanting to hold her close to our hearts. To rock her back and forth and allow her desperate need for love to weave into our longing to give love. Analeigh and Jenco had never been foster parents before, but they soon took Ada in as their own.

Around that same time, a boy named Bongani showed up at Project Heal in the middle of the night. He had been beaten and bruised by his drunken mother. She misplaced her purse and thought that Bongani stole it from her. This wasn't the first time Bongani was beaten by his mother while she was under the influence of alcohol. Without any other place to go, he walked from the village to Project Heal. *Safety.* The number one thing these kids wanted was safety. With all the items I had written down on my piece of paper to make an excellent prom, I had to add one more thing: Transportation. It wasn't safe for the kids to walk alone during the daytime, much less during the nighttime after prom.

With my list of items, I put my hands over it and prayed, "God, I don't know how all of these things are going to happen, but I believe that you can make them happen. I choose to trust in you."

I called restaurants, chefs, photographers, grocery stores, flower shops, churches, and friends of my housemates to ask for donations. The first person to say "yes" was an Italian chef. He donated two types of pasta with salad and buttery garlic bread. The dresses came trickling in from Analeigh's friends and local dress shops. Some women donated up to twelve dresses themselves. There were no lack in dresses. A woman from a local church donated her time to decorate. Another woman donated flowers from her shop and yet another donated decorations from her wedding. In the final weeks, my mother decided to fly across the world to be there for the prom day.

The girls arrived in the early afternoon giddy with excitement on the day of the prom. First, they went to the garage—which was transformed into a beauty salon. With their hair and make-up professionally done, they went to another area to pick out their favorite dress. If you've ever watched a girl pick something out, it's pretty clear if she likes it or not. It was a beautiful process to watch the girls pick out different dresses and try them on, not giving up until they found the perfect one. With the onset of golden hour, the photographer arrived and led the girls to an open field to snap all kinds of Beyoncè-status, fabulous photos. If we didn't usher the girls to dinner, I believe they would have snapped photos in that yellow-dry field with strong trees in the background until the final droplets of light gave way to the dark night.

One doesn't know to be thankful for all they have, I pondered, until they see what it looks like to not have. I was terrified I wouldn't have a date to prom—*years* before prom was even an option. These girls didn't have the opportunity to attend such an event. The difference made me feel guilty and thankful. Guilty for my self-centeredness. And thankful for the opportunity to experience this. The night was better than my own prom.

All of that stressing, anxiety-filled days, and fears I had placed on myself about "being cool" and "having a cool date" just really didn't matter.

In Xhosa culture, women are supposed to serve the men. They are viewed as lower in class, and many women are unaware of their own rights. Basic rights to their freedom, choices, and their own bodies, which is why the Masikanye group existed. One of the young men, he was maybe eighteen years old, decided to volunteer his time to teach the young boys from the village a different way of being. His name was Ndivho, it means "knowledge." Ndivho began to meet with the boys who visited the program that were of similar age to the girls. Although, this prom was technically a "female only" prom, the boys decided to be a part of it—and serve the girls dinner. Ndivho helped dress the boys in tuxes, with hand-sewn bowties of all different colors and designs.

The garage was transformed from a cold cement building to a gorgeous ballroom. The walls and windows were hung with light purple and white drapes. A variety of flowers from a local flower shop were elegantly placed on the long table of food, on circular dining tables, and in standing vases. A makeshift dance floor, with a volunteer DJ, greeted the girls as they were ushered in by the gentlemen in suits and homemade bowties. Ndivho stood at the door, glowingly proud of his group of young men.

Before dinner, one of the "mamas," as we called them, gave me a microphone to pray. Humbled, I thanked God for this evening to celebrate these young women. My mother got to be a part of the evening, and enjoyed the simple joy of their culture.

It wasn't all joy for my mother's visit, however. One evening we packed onto a bus headed into Mazamomhle because I wanted to show my mother this church. To introduce her to the people I felt spirit to spirit connected to, even though I didn't know their language. There were no doors on the bus, it was like an extended fourteen-passenger van. Stains on the seats and more than one person sitting where one should fit. Mamas had bags and bags of groceries they held closely to their core. Teenage boys played music loudly on their busted-up phones with wires sticking out. I was amazed that the things still worked. The sun was falling behind the village as we drove in. A few lone lights lit the faces of people walking by. Men walked in groups. Women walked in groups. Nobody walked alone.

We arrived at a vacant school building and waited and waited. Not a single person from the church showed up. A woman who works at Project Heal saw my mother and I sitting outside the building and said, "They must've decided not to meet tonight. It's late now, pull your sweatshirt over your head and tighten the strings so people cannot see the color of your skin."

My mother had on a long coat that couldn't cover her face.

The woman said, "Just don't make eye contact with anyone. If they see you are white, it might not end well."

We followed this woman to a shack. The door was a piece of scrap metal, which she moved aside to reveal one woman and two children sitting in the open space on one dusty couch. The floor was dirt with a circular rug covering the central area. I felt as soon as we walked through the entrance, that this location wasn't any safer than being out in the open. Now we were trapped. We couldn't go anywhere from this container. With the entrance open, two men came to the doorway and rapped on the side of the shack. They said something in Xhosa to the women. One of the women responded, and the three of them conversed for a few minutes.

Outside of the shack, wires trailed through puddles of water from a dimming streetlight to the single hanging bulb giving light in the shack. As the conversation between the three heightened, the light source went out. Complete blackness, in the entire shack.

Here is the moment. I thought my life would end after falling out of the tree, not here in a shack in South Africa. My mother prayed quietly next to me. A pang of guilt hit my stomach as I knew we didn't need to be in this position. It was my lack of judgement that got us here—in an extremely dangerous situation. We held onto hands, and I tried to think what to do when they came for me. Do I fight? Do I allow them to do whatever they want and not resist? Will they let us live?

There was a moment of silence, and then, they left. The light came back on. I tried to read the faces of the little girls to see if they were scared. Having no idea what conversation just happened, I did know that we needed to get out of there. The woman from Project Heal looked at me and said, "Is there anyone you can call to get out of here?"

I used her cell phone to call Jenco, one of my housemates.

"Can you possibly come get my mother and me?"

"Where are you?"

"Mzamomhle, near the school."

"What! Stay where you are. I'm on my way."

Fifteen minutes later, Jenco came driving into the village and we got in, releasing tension. He gave us a stern talking to, letting us know, once again, that the village is not safe—especially for white people at night.

Driving out of the village, I watched groups of faces lit under the sparse streetlights, just like the way it was driving in. My mind ran with how different their life circumstances were from mine. I could be rescued out of the village, returned to a safe home, and at any point, could return to the safest country on the planet.

The unfairness moved me to question a just God. And what was I doing here in this impoverished place, thinking that I could help? Me— a twenty-one-year-old college student. All of this made me truly angry, and yet I still chose to wake up at five a.m. most mornings and devote the first few hours to prayer. Fervent prayer that the God of the heavens would move in Mzamomhle, heal the broken, remove the abuse, and provide a brighter day for their future. I prayed safety over Mzamomhle. I prayed for all of the children like Bongani to gain the courage to run away and never come back. For all of the women trapped without knowledge of their own rights, to run away. But where could these souls go?

As part of my mother's visit, we booked a week at a resort in Morgan Bay. Rocky cliffs jutted up against crashing waves and leveled out to sugar-sand. The resort was all-inclusive with five-course meals served twice a day. Breakfast with a five-course meal? I didn't even know that was a thing. A rooftop bar with lounge chairs revealed a breathtaking view of the ocean. There was horseback riding, rock climbing, mountain biking, and beach yoga. A dreamer's paradise getaway.

Privilege. I didn't have the word for it at the time, but I was feeling the effects of white privilege. I had the opportunity to travel across the seas, volunteer my time, and then end the trip with a week-long stay at a luxurious resort right on the oceanside. I looked around at the clear line between those with opportunity and those with a lack of opportunity. All of the servers were Black. All of the owners were white. All of the people with smiling faces, who made my breakfast, swapped out clean towels in the middle of the day, and asked "ma'am, can I get you anything?" were all Black. But the positions that required a little bit of education or background, such as the climbing guide and the bartender—white. Now, what could I do about this? Shame myself for being white? Shame myself for having this privilege? Shame myself for thinking that I could do *anything* to make lasting change in this divided nation?

It was wintertime in South Africa when we visited Morgan Bay. The waves were a little harsher, and the wind had a bite. It wasn't cold, just a little chilly. Not beach weather. I went for a walk along the water's edge and listened to the continual lap, and I asked God, "Why is it this way?"

Before I purchased my second return flight from South Africa, I had a very serious moment with myself in an office-turned-makeshift-gym that was adjacent to the couple's house I was renting. Pedaling and pedaling on an old spin bike, I asked God, "Should I commit my life to this village? Stay here and make another nonprofit like Project Heal on the other side of the village?"

Listening to God is sometimes like hearing a single sound in a crowd of people and trying to guess which person it came from. Was this me or you? A dream for myself or a dream for someone else? I decided to stick to it and even tell Cindy on Monday.

Cindy came rolling up in her white bucky. She always had a knitted basket with her. Inside her basket could be coloring pages for the kids teaching about their rights and crayons mixed with pages for a new grant she was writing and an agenda for a board meeting. She covered all bases in that little basket with the circle handles.

"I think I'm going to drop out of college completely, and move here," I said.

"What will you do?" Cindy asked.

"Help you. Maybe start another nonprofit on the other side of Mzamomhle."

"You can't do that," Cindy said. "You need to return to America and finish your education."

"But, why? It all feels so meaningless there. Here—you are changing lives. You are transforming an entire generation. You are doing something worth living for."

"Do you know why these children are living in poverty, Emilee?"

Silence.

"You have access to the one thing that would remove every single person from poverty—education," Cindy said. "You must return to

America, finish your education, and then you can make change in the world."

My mother and I, after our resort stay, packed up our suitcases and returned to the airport. I had long braids down to my little-bit-thicker waist from all the African rice, beans, and meat of the past seven months, and a piece of paper declaring that I had extended my visa. Except the piece of paper meant nothing to the immigration officer.

A woman of about forty-five years old in a uniform opened my passport and said, "You stay too long."

"Yes, but there's the papers showing that I got clearance to stay longer."

"No, this not work. Come with me."

My heart began to race, imagining that I would be beaten and all of my possessions stolen. She took me to a back room with white walls. There was one card table with a printer sitting on it and a stack of papers next to it. Two of the exact same sign hung on the wall showing two Black hands exchanging money with a large red "x" over the hands. The sign read "Don't Do Corruption."

I stood there and waited and waited. Another man came into the room that was clearly Zimbabwean. He had a small leather bag and a wore a wool sweater that looked like it had lasted him for the past twenty years. His face wrought with pain and hopelessness. The man stared at the floor, and so I decided to do the same. The flooring was some sort of fake tile that felt like standing on plastic.

Breaking the silence, the printer woke up with flashing lights and spit out four pages. The man and I watched the four pages roll out one by one. Soon after, a heavy-set officer walked in and handed two of them to me and two to the other man. They had our recorded information on them from our passports. The man stamped each of them with a stamp that said something in Swahili. I had no idea what it said, but the other man broke down in tears when he read it. I had an urge to hug him and console him, though I didn't know what was happening. Are we going to jail?

The officer said, "Five years, you leave this country and do not come back. Five years."

Banned

I was banned from South Africa for five years. The place I was contemplating moving to for life, I could no longer visit for five years. The Zimbabwean and I walked out with our new papers of rejection, and I told my mother the news. I wondered about this man's story: what was he leaving behind? Was his family in South Africa? His wife? Children? Once we made it to our gate, I doubled over, dropping my backpack, and cried. Both for myself and this man who appeared as if his entire life had just been ripped away from him. For both of us, South Africa was no longer an option. Dead and gone. Not. An. Option.

Just Head West

Somehow, I had to make peace with my life in America again. I returned to college, graduated in 2015, and met a very nice man whom I planned to marry one day—it seemed like the logical thing to do next. Go to college (check), get married (unchecked).

His name was Mike. He had olive skin, coffee-bean brown eyes, and was going to school for engineering. He was a very impressive rock climber and super-Christian. We spent one year together until I graduated and decided to pack up my car and move West. I needed something new, but I promised him that I would return a year later and we'd get married.

With our collective deep roots in Christian teaching, we knew to remain pure and prepare for marriage; to "save ourselves," if you know what I mean. Mike and I started reading marriage books together, and had mentors that helped us along in our courtship. Mike, however, was two years younger. I had no plans of actually leaving him, just for the time being. I would come back. But as it turns out, the West truly does change people. Or maybe the Lord that glued us together just failed to mention we wouldn't stick forever.

Two months prior to my graduation, I received a call from my cousin living in Sun Valley, Idaho. Avia was the one person in the family I saw the most of myself in. She had lived in Montana, and now Idaho, with stories of ski trips and backpacking in the mountains. She was living the outdoor adventure lifestyle I so desired. Over the years we tried to connect, but failed to actually make any plans a go. She told me on the phone that she had a potential job opportunity for me: to work as a wilderness therapy guide.

Avia is a therapist, who also worked in wilderness therapy at the time. She said they needed field guides. The position's schedule was fourteen days in the field with teenagers struggling with a variety of issues, and then fourteen days off. The field director, Brent, was a small-boned man with more heart than sternness. Even though he was less than intimidating, he was still the one in charge of hiring me, and I felt like I needed to toughen up. I wore loose hiking pants, a knife on my belt, a fitted t-shirt, and ball cap during our interview—which took place in the desert.

The desert. Not the Sahara-type, with the camels and hot Arabian sun, that's not the type of desert we're working with here. The desert in Idaho is high-desert, with dry land that stretches for miles and miles teeming with sagebrush, rattlesnakes, and sandstone canyons.

The program was called WildRidge Wilderness Therapy. It's based in Dot, Idaho, where there's one bar, train tracks, and if you're lucky, you'll see a tumbleweed roll by both. Avia lived an hour-and-a-half north of Dot in a truly magical mountain town called Sun Valley, Idaho. She took me in during my transition, and helped me get accustomed to my new life. Avia had a roommate at the time that was about fifty years old named Kim. She was a pilot and out to prove something great about herself to anyone who would listen to her.

Our conversation revolved around her telling me how important she was, in regards to some wildlife study she was involved in. She flew over vast landscapes and scanned it to count a specific species of wildlife. Maybe fish or deer. It was less of a conversation and more of a one-sided telling. Kim was shorter in stature with rough skin, and wavy strings of hair that puffed over her shoulders in frizz. She was popping in the dating world, sometimes going on multiple dates in a day. I didn't understand how there were enough men in a town of 2,500 people to make that happen, but she did.

On the Fourth of July, I had my first breakdown in Idaho. Avia was gone and I was at the house with Kim. I told her I thought I'd drive up the Valley and go get a drink. Maybe just have a Fourth of July drink by myself.

"If you drive and have even an ounce of alcohol today, you must go five under the speed limit. The cops are all over this valley and *will* pull you over."

I decided to have one beer at the house, and then I cried. Alone again. I was alone again, picturing all of my family and friends enjoying the fireworks and laughter back home. I was twenty-two years old, and didn't even realize that I had the power to make my own choices. If an older adult (Kim, in this circumstance) told me to do something, I better listen and do as they tell me to do.

Two weeks later, Avia and I were helping clean the house and I was given this very odd-looking vacuum. It was in multiple parts, and so I asked her how to put it together. Her response, "If you can't figure that out, I don't know how you expect to make it very far in life."

The words stunned me, and made me completely defenseless. I walked outside and cried, disappointed that I did not stick up for myself and for allowing her to push me around. *An adult told me I won't make it very far in life, this must be the truth because adults know everything.* I felt I had to go along with whatever this woman said: she owned the house I was staying in for the time being. There was no other place for me to go, so I must be nice and listen to all she tells me to do and how to feel about myself.

I sat there, with tears in my eyes, putting this stupid vacuum together. Kim walked by, scanning over me, proud to prove her dominance. This was a pattern, before I knew what a pattern was, that I'd discover about myself over time. Emilee chooses the "nice girl" route. Emilee will always get pushed around. She won't speak up for herself. She will do what others want. She doesn't see her value or know her worth; she waits for others to show it to her. The only problem is that I had to discover nobody else would show me my worth. Nobody else was sticking up for me.

How Do I Stop Making Myself So Small?

The events with Kim triggered a line of uncomfortable moments in time where I laid myself down to be someone else's doormat. It angered me, but how would I change? I cared too much about what others thought of me. I chose to be stepped on, so that I wouldn't risk being disliked. People like people who bow to them.

By the time my first shift for wilderness therapy came around, I was glad to get away from Kim. But what was waiting for me in the desert, I discovered, may have been worse.

WildRidge was sort of a new company that had morphed from an old company. New name, with people not so new to the game. They functioned out of an abandoned hospital at the time. The entrance was two sets of heavy hospital doors leading to an open space with one large round table, topographical maps on the walls, and gnarled blue carpet. The spirit in this place wasn't exactly warming, or even welcoming.

Here I met my first group of instructors, who were a granola-type of people. Looking around the room, I noticed only three other women. Most of the instructors were men. And they all appeared to be tougher than me. Looking back, I suppose it wasn't instructors I should have been afraid of, but the students.

Brent came walking in and gave us the overview of the kids in the field.

"We just got a six-foot-three, seventeen-year-old boy in this morning that is not happy to be here. He was brought in by transporters this morning, and attacked three staff personnel," Brent said. "I got punched."

One of the guy instructors came walking out of the kitchen, barefoot, eating mixed greens directly out of the plastic container they came in.

"Well, shit," he said in-between bites, "this is gonna be one crazy shift."

His name was Anthony. He had curly hair, gentle eyes, and the defined body of a true adventurer. On his fingers were rings displaying yoga symbols and on his wrists were braided bracelets like the ones you make at summer camp as a kid.

At the time, there were three groups we could be put in to: the girls, the boys, and a third group we affectionately called the "wild hares." The girls' and the boys' groups were ages fifteen to eighteen. The wild hares were the most challenging rascals of a group—boys, ages eleven to fourteen. There was no list of supplies to purchase or way to know what to prepare for in the field. I packed rubber gardening boots, jeans, a flannel, baseball cap, my new sleeping bag, sleeping pad, and a tent into a large red backpack. The morning of my first shift, I drank as much coffee as I could, knowing I had to go on a fourteen-day coffee cleanse after that. And also not realizing that the other instructors were well prepared for their coffee addictions, bringing their very own wilderness French presses and coffee from organic markets in Boise.

Dirt kicked up in clouds as we drove into the desert where our groups and several burned-out instructors were waiting for us. Twenty-five minutes later, our fifteen-passenger van was parked on a flat desert area surrounded by deep, red canyons. Ten tents were set-up in a circle, all the same shade of orange. A make-shift kitchen area with a stove and picnic table was set up adjacent to the tents. Long white strings tied down a white tarp meant to protect them from intense winds. The stakes had large rocks placed over them, and the tarp, just like everything else, was dusted with desert-dry dirt. A man with a long scraggily beard came running to the van as if we were his saviors. Anthony hopped out and hugged him.

They exchanged notes about the boys in the group, all of them somewhere along their roughly ninety-day journey in the desert. And then we took the old instructors, dusted with dirt and heavy with tired faces. Anthony and two other instructors were left behind. Next, was the girls' group—my stop. The groups were about a ten minutes' drive in the desert apart. Driving over a hillside, I could see that this camp had parameters, made up of barbed wire. Within the confines of the barbed wire, was a circular yurt (canvas-domed shelter), another grouping of orange tents, an outhouse, and a cemented area for the kitchen. Each group had a head instructor, which was the leader. For my group, it was Candice. She was tall and big-boned, had long, thick caramel hair, and possessed a strong presence. I felt like a little fly in her wolf-like dominion. The girls flocked to her and welcomed her, as if she was a celebrity. Besides Candice and myself, we had one guy instructor in our group named William. He was thin, tall, and tattooed, with light blue dreamy eyes and blond hair. On the drive out to the desert, he sang, awkwardly, on key and loudly, exclaiming that he was in *a cappella* in college. He had just graduated from college the year prior, like myself.

William, I could feel, wanted attention from us—the female instructors. Sitting in the back of the van, William in the middle with his angelic voice and face, I made the decision that I would give him as little attention as possible. Turns out, that's exactly the type of reaction that draws guys like him towards girls like me.

"Let's meet for a quick group to get to know the girls," Candice said.

The girls looked like inmates in bright orange and sometimes red clothing, strategically dressed so that if they decided to run away—we would be able to spot them for miles and miles in the hot desert distance. I wasn't so concerned for their safety as I was my own. Our group had twelve girls. There were only three of us, and if I had to choose someone to protect us all, it would be Candice. Not William.

Standing in a circle with the entire group, we made our introductions. I stood tall and tried to take my dominion like Candice's seemingly easy expression of hers, but I felt so small. So incapable of holding space for these girls. Would they even listen to me or just roll their eyes and do what they wanted? Will I even be able to make it at this job?

My stomach twisted in knots of anxious energy. I listened to each of the girls share where they're from, why they're here, and what they're working on. We shared the same about ourselves as instructors. When the circle landed on William, I learned even more about him and that I, also, wanted nothing to do with him.

"Hello ladies, my name is William…" he started, even him using the term "ladies" and his full name annoyed me.

"I'm from New York, and I just graduated from college last year with a degree in psychology. I played soccer in college, and I really enjoy being outdoors. You are the reason I am here, and I'm excited to be out in the desert with you."

I smiled and listened patiently, making sure to let my eyes drift with the next speaker and not remain on him. Each girl's demeanor was directly proportionate to the amount of time they had spent in the desert up until that point. The ones that had been there for a few months had a rhythm to them, they could stand tall and introduce themselves accordingly. They were also well-versed in the wilderness terms and skills, such as building a fire with a bow-drill set. I didn't even know what a bow-drill set was, but I too would have to learn how to make a fire using only the elements in the desert if I wanted to become a head instructor.

Then, it was my turn.

"Hey, everyone, my name is Emilee. I'm from Minnesota, and this is my first shift. I have a degree in creative writing, and I enjoy rock climbing. It is my choice to be here, and I know it is not your choice to be here—but I hope you'll allow me to be a part of your journey in the desert."

As soon as I finished my introduction, I questioned it. I have a degree in *creative writing*? Who cares? Again, their facial expressions to my introduction perfectly reflected where they were at in their growth journey. The new girls barely even looked my direction. The seasoned ones listened intently, and even nodded along and smiled.

William's eyes remained on me, as the group's shifted to the girl beside me. I wanted to mouth "fuck off," but I smiled sweetly instead. The fact that he knew he was attractive just *pissed me off*, and I wasn't going to give him the attention he had most likely received his whole life.

As soon as the next girl began to speak, the fourteen-passenger van rumbled by behind her back to "base," as we called it. This is really it now, it's just me and the group. The van has left the desert. The girls' introductions softened my heart, as I realized most of them were simply dealing with insecurities. Body image issues, boy issues, food issues, mental health issues, and one thing I had zero experience with—cutting.

I couldn't help but notice the last girl's wrists as she shared about her hometown in California. Her name was Kenzie, and she had long blonde hair that danced down her shoulders like the waters of the California coast. She was outfitted with a red sweatshirt that was too large for her. When she spoke, the sleeves slipped up to her elbows, revealing slashes on both wrists. I was so naïve of cutting at the time, that I strained my eyes to see what was going on. Was it some sort of henna tattoo? How does one get marks or scars on their arms like that?

By cutting themselves. Kenzie was a "Level II" risk. This meant, I, or another instructor, had to be within arm's length distance from her at all times. If Kenzie was out of sight, she had to count so we always knew where she was. Like in the bathroom, for instance, she had to count the entire time she was in there. Kenzie was an easy Level II; she actually wanted the closeness. She would ask me to go with her places, instead of testing the boundaries and dashing away. She was quiet, kind, and curious. But the fact that she had landed herself in wilderness therapy, thousands of miles away from her hometown, told me she had a dark side. It took a while to come out.

Every night we had "group" around the campfire, checking in with each student. They took turns sharing how they were feeling, what they were challenged by, and sometimes, one student would get the "talking stick" for the entire night and they'd share their life story. The challenge here was to share as authentically and honestly as they could with their desert peers what it was that got them here. Kenzie's story was captivating.

In the glow of the firelight, propped perfectly in her chair, Kenzie shared everything.

"I was raped when I was fifteen years old by a guy that I didn't know," Kenzie started. "It was at a random party that I went to with my friends, and he forced me to have sex with him. It was painful and I hated it," she started to tear up. "I was so ashamed that I didn't tell my parents, and then I stopped getting my period. I went to a gas station and bought a pregnancy test… and it was positive."

She paused here, collapsing forward in her chair, crying and covering her face.

"My parents have a lot of money and they wanted me to go to really nice school and all this, and if I had this baby, I knew I couldn't go. So, I went to a clinic alone and got an abortion. My parents still don't know."

Kenzie was seventeen at the time, and I grew all the closer to her. Feeling for her pain, and then I was slapped with my naïveté again. After the girls went to bed, the instructors stayed up each night for "debrief." This is where we'd discuss the day, what went well and what didn't go well, and how we can better support one another.

"You believed her story?" Candice asked, giving me a bogus look.

"Why wouldn't I believe her story?"

"Looking at her charts, she pulls shit like this all the time just to get attention. That story was completely made up."

My mind spun with confusion. What if her story was real? What if the problem is that nobody believes her? Or maybe it was completely made up, and I'm still naïve. My first shift in the field felt like a bitch slap, showing me how little I knew. The days drug on, and then all at once, they were suddenly over, and that same janky van rolled out to the desert to pick us up.

14 Days On – 14 Days Off

We were the last group to get picked up, so all the other guides were already packed in. Anthony was closest to the door and opened it wide before the van stopped. He was yelling that we had made it. On the bumpy drive back to headquarters, Anthony announced that he was going to Banff, Canada, to climb some mountains. Ironically, I had already made plans to meet up with Mike in Canada during his family's annual trip. I planned to meet up with Mike, but now, I could also go with Anthony and top-out on some rad mountains.

"You're really going to Banff?" I said.

"Yeah girrrrl," Anthony said, shaking his head of gorgeous locks up and down.

"Can I come with?"

"Seriously? You wanna go?" he said, astonished.

"Yes! I was already planning to go to Canada, but now I have an even better reason."

"Fuck yeah, let's roll. Let's meet at the welcome center near Banff."

A moment on the word *fuck*. Being raised in Minnesota, where people apologize for their foul language when they say "damn" or "hell," I had never been amongst a community that used the word "fuck," until I moved out west—where it was a commonly used adjective. I began to notice that people who had gone through intense things in life, used an intense language. The tougher the crowd, the rougher the language.

So, just like that, I was headed to Canada to visit my boyfriend and his family, and climb massive mountain peaks with a friend I had just met. I didn't have service in Canada, so I turned my phone on airplane mode, and found WIFI connection to message Anthony to tell him I had arrived at the welcome center. It was a beautiful structure with cases and cases of maps. Roll out maps, old maps, topographical maps, digital maps. You-name-it maps, they were there.

Anthony rolled up, windows down, yelling at me, "We in Canada, girrrllll!"

Knowing the depth of his free-spirit-ness, I was nervous he had gotten lost or forgot or just wouldn't show up. But here he was. Anthony hopped out of his Volkswagen named "Brenda" and said, "Let's go find some mountains to climb."

It took us two days of researching the maps to really decide on one mountain. It was called Old Goat Mountain in Alberta, Canada. It stood to 10,236 feet in elevation and was not a commonly climbed route. In fact, we couldn't find information of anyone climbing it at all. With his dirt-caked fingers, Anthony traced the topographical map of Old Goat Mountain and made sketchy remarks like "We should probably be able to climb that section, it's a 5.8? Maybe a 5.8. Can you climb a 5.8?"

"Yeah, I can climb a 5.8," I said.

"And this section," he carried on, "looks like it cliffs off, but we should be able to drop down into this crevasse or double belay down from this peak to this peak...."

This thing sounded dreadful. I had never double belayed. What does that even look like?

We spent two nights in the national forest in our tents. There were signs everywhere that said we can't camp in the National Forest just anywhere, we had to stay in the designated spots. Which, were $30 a night. Anthony wasn't gonna have that. Not with his Volkswagen beater set-up complete with blow-up sleeping pad, backpacking stove, organic noodles, organic vegetables he scored at a CO-OP on the way there, and plenty of hoppy IPA beers. We found a random parking lot and hiked into the forest, camping beside a shallow riverbed. Every movement of sound I heard in the forest that night, I was sure, was a cop hiking out to tell us hippies we can't camp here.

Anthony and I had a lot in common, and a few of those things got us in deep trouble on this adventure. The first one was time; a mystical existence of something that runs the world, but we just couldn't seem to grasp. We woke up, made coffee, and drove to the mountain to check it out in daylight one last time before committing. Then, we purified enough water for the day hike, made deliciously thick crunchy peanut butter and raspberry jelly sandwiches, two Jetboils of coffee, and visited with the camp host at the base of Old Goat Mountain.

We parked my car at the start and his at the finish, on the opposite end of the mountain. The vehicles were about five miles apart. The camp host, Amy, told us that her and her husband had been camp hosts there for over ten years and hadn't known of anyone to climb the mountain. That was surprising to me, and made me want to re-think our decision to try to summit this thing—with a start time just beyond noon.

"If that car right there," Anthony said, pointing to my car, "is still here tomorrow by two p.m., something went wrong and send for help."

We gave them emergency numbers— OUR MOTHERS' PHONE NUMBERS, which, we came to realize later, was a terrible idea.

The camp host looked concerned, but agreed to the plan.

"Alright, you kids stay safe up there," Amy said.

We walked back to my car, grabbed our packs, and started up the steep mountainside. The top of the mountain was a grey swath of color, I couldn't quite make out the peak's form. It just looked like a lot of rock. Our dusty feet went from gravel to grassland to forested mountainside within one hour. Anthony stopped at every mushroom and butterfly he found intriguing. I was set on hiking up this thing—on the final destination. He was more about the journey. There was no path, but we didn't have any trouble weaving in and out of the pine trees, breathing in the ease of the mid-summer air.

Anthony brought a small camera and paused to take several photos of the scene around us. I felt like daylight was a measurement we needed to pay attention to, as it was now well into the afternoon and we hadn't even made it to the ridgeline.

"Look at all those gorgeous mountain peaks!" Anthony said, pausing with his arms open wide like all the "You Can Do Anything" posters I'd seen in stores growing up. This was real life. The mountain peaks were snowcapped, with a dusting of ice and snow that layered off to reveal perfectly placed trees studding the mid to lower half of the mountain range. At the bottom was an aqua blue lake, irresistibly glowing in the afternoon sun.

Soon, the pine trees holding crisp air disappeared and it was just thin air, rock, and sky. The mountainside went from gradual to straight up.

The time for the "can you climb a 5.8?" had arrived. We carefully placed our hands and feet, balancing not only the weight of our bodies, but also the weight of our packs, up this cliffside. Step by step, I knew I could go up. My body craved the forward motion, the grip and pull of each hold. My mind relished in the concentration it takes to ensure you'll make it to the next hold. The one thing I knew I couldn't do—was climb back down. Down-climbing a section you can climb up are two very different things. I was truly committed to this mountainside, where there was no return route.

The sun was now quickly descending down the backside of the mountain. I wanted to move fast, I felt we *needed* to move fast. The top of the mountain was a knife ridge, with jagged rocks jutting out on either side. Slate rock flanked the east and west sides of the mountain, which would make a slippery slope all the way down the mountainside if one of our feet were to slip. I gripped the mountain's peak with both hands, and stuck the flat of my boots on either side of the mountain—crawling along as fast as I could. Anthony was a few paces behind, still pausing to balance on the knife ridge to capture a few photos.

"Well, shit, girl, you're a great mountain climber! Just cruisin' along!" Anthony said, all relaxed.

"I'm nervous we won't have enough time to get down this thing."

"Just keep going! We'll get down, no worries."

I took a few deep breaths and then said he should lead for a while.

"Okay, cool! Let's roll!' Anthony and I held onto each other as he shifted to the front of the ridge, and I followed behind, watching his every move.

And then, the moment arrived. The true moment. The mountainside completely cliffed off, as we were afraid of when researching Old Goat Mountain.

"There it is," Anthony said, somewhat looking excited. "You still got that rope in your backpack?"

"Yeah," I said.

"Great, take it out. We're gonna double rappel down this thing."

The sun that was once a brilliant yellow circle in the sky was now melting into a mixed magenta-orange color. The color of the setting sun, releasing daylight and giving into the cold of the night. We unpacked our harnesses and added a few layers to our bodies. When one person rappels down a mountainside, a wooden wall, or a brick building—they typically loop both sides of the rope through their belay device that's attached to their harness. A belay device is an aluminum safety device that looks like a toaster with two slots for the rope to go through. When you're belaying someone normally, the rope connects you to the climber, and you, as the belayer, are the break. When you *double* rappel, you both get one side of the rope that's connected to a focal point–in this case, the peak of a mountain. It's less safe, but if you do it right, it's a viable option to get from one peak to the next.

With about six inches of space between our belay devices attaching the rope to the peak, we balanced each other's weight on each side of the rope.

"Alright, pull tight, stand up straight against the rock, like you're trying to push away from the mountain," Anthony said.

He mirrored me until the rope was taut, and we were ready to double belay down to the next peak, about fifteen feet. His feet touched the ridge first, and mine second. We held onto the rope as we both regained our balance on the next section of Old Goat Mountain's ridgeline.

"Aw, fuck yeah, nice work!" Anthony said.

He went to pull the rope down and there was no give. The rope was stuck. We took turns yanking and yanking on the thing. No. Give.

"Let's just leave the rope," I said.

"No, I don't think that's a good idea," Anthony said. "What if we need it again?"

"The sun is setting fast, and it's starting to get cold."

"I think I can free climb back up to that peak and get it," he said.

"What? Are you serious?"

Any single misstep or broken rock would send him tumbling down the rocky mountainside. Before I could convince him otherwise, he had dropped his backpack and was climbing up the fifteen feet section we had just rappelled down. I stood there, hands sweating and heart pounding, watching him gracefully move up the wall, unhook the rope, wrap it around his shoulders, and just as gracefully, climb back down.

The rope had a huge cut in it from us trying to free it from the sharp rock.

"Shit, that doesn't look good," he said, in reference to the frayed rope. "But I think it's still usable."

I curled the rope up, put it in my backpack, and quickly sank from confidence to complete panic. Where I was cruising along the ridgeline an hour earlier, I couldn't bring myself to make another move across this new ridge. There were even greater danger zones, with jagged rock and bits missing. Clear cut-outs of sections that had broken off and the remains were somewhere, thousands of feet, down the mountainside. I pictured my thin body tumbling down the mountainside, with my heavy red backpack smacking cliff after cliff. I froze.

"Em, we gotta keep goin', the sun's really setting now."

I shook my head and began to tear up.

"I can't keep going."

He turned around and noticed in my face that I was serious, I had turned to a stone of sheer panic. Anthony held my shoulders and said, "Look at me, we are going to make it down off this thing, we just need to keep moving."

"Right foot here," he said, pointing to where I should step next. "Left hand here. Good. Left foot here..."

We went on like that until we made it to a wider section, where I could finally walk without balancing on little rocks here and there and just praying to God they'd hold.

Standing side by side, we watched the sun disappear, rotating around the earth's surface and leaving us in the dark. We searched for our headlamps. Collectively, we had one with a dying battery. We had run out of water, and when we went to at least find the sandwiches we had packed, noticed that we had left those behind too. A large glacier sat just a few hundred feet below us, revealing the temperature was low enough to maintain its icy structure.

I sat down and sobbed. We were going to die up here. There was no escape route. The sunlight was gone. I took out all of my layers and we made a "worst-case scenario" plan.

"I think I hear something dripping over there," Anthony said, pointing to a little caved-in part of the mountain. "Let's go see if we can get some water."

We held out our Nalgene water bottles and captured the water, drip by drip. Barely gathering enough for a full sip.

"We're going to have to sleep up here," he said.

I was already shaking from the wind and cold. Could our bodies actually make it through the night? We found a section of the mountainside, a ledge of about five feet in width, where we decided to lay down and take shelter against the night.

"I know you've got your boyfriend and everything, but we might need body heat just to make it through this," Anthony said.

Through chattering teeth, I said, "Yes, get over here."

We cuddled harder than infatuated lovers and wrapped our backpacks' rain covers around our faces to trap some heat in. We used my climbing rope to cover our bodies. And we shook, and shook, and froze, and shook some more. When our limbs began to go numb, we stood up and did jumping jacks to heat back up. Standing thousands of feet up in the air, on an exposed mountainside, doing jumping jacks to stay warm, we both began to laugh. Frozen, painful laughs.

The sun rose just after four a.m., staining the night's lavender sky with a magenta-orange sunrise. He held out his phone to see if he could get service... nothing.

"We gotta bail off the backside this thing," he said, pulling his buff over his face and corralling his curls back.

By this point, I had become an Athena of the Mountainside, just ready to take on any sort of trial and war to get down. I put on a baseball cap and said, "Let's do this."

The sun spent little time heating the rocky cliff face, as we peddled our feet back and forth in heavy scree rock down the backside of Old Goat Mountain. A few hundred feet down, we paused and noticed a mountain goat standing proudly over its dominion.

"He's saying to us that we were no match for this mountain," Anthony said. "This is his mountain."

Mountain goats move gracefully from cliff to cliff. He stood proud, with his horns rolling like cycles of wisdom next to pronounced face. We took a moment to thank the goat for being there and reminding us that we're human. We felt very human: thirsty, hungry, tired, and dazed. Our muscles were shaking, and any fat that we had somehow acquired from burgers and beers in the few days before we left, were no longer in the reserves.

It took us a few hours to make it out of the scree rock section and into the forested part of Old Goat Mountain. Except this time, all of the timber had fallen. Instead of hiking effortlessly through life-giving pine trees as we did on the way up, we were now climbing over and under log after log. It sapped my energy even further, and my mind began to slip from reality.

"Come on, Em," Anthony said. "We need to keep moving."

Just as he started to encourage me to move faster, we heard the unmistakable sound of wind whipping through sharp blades in the sky. Search and Rescue. It was twelve minutes past two in the afternoon.

"Fuck, there they are." Anthony said. "They're looking for us."

The timber was so dense that they couldn't see us. The chopper circled and circled, crossing our path dozens of times, but unable to find us.

"We've gotta move faster so they know we're alive," Anthony said.

I rapped down hard on the buckles on my backpack and tapped into some other level of energy to get myself through this. Hunger is an uncomfortable feeling, but lacking water and trying to push your body is a whole different thing. My mouth was dry and cottony.

We finally made it to a service road next to the aqua blue lake we had seen from the mountainside. I wanted to drop my pack, run to the water, and lap it up like a dog. Anthony warned me that we could get giardia, a parasite in untreated water that causes diarrhea for weeks and even further dehydration. As we kneeled beside the glistening lake, I desperately wanted to sneak a sip, just one sip, from the blue restorative liquid. What were the odds that I'd get giardia? It's not like Anthony seeing if I took a sip would determine if I got giardia or not, but I felt so weak and unable to stick to the rules. We filled our water bottles with the lake water and added tablets to treat it. It takes about thirty minutes to treat the water, I felt like I physically couldn't wait that long.

"We gotta keep moving," Anthony said.

For a hippy-man who is always so relaxed, once he knew Search and Rescue was after us, he was not relaxed. We needed to get back to the beginning. We kept on hiking with our water bottles sloshing around lake water and slowly dissolving the tablets.

A large white truck came rolling down the service road and a woman rolled down the window, "Are you Anthony and Emilee?"

"Yes," we said, feeling relieved and ashamed.

The woman spoke into a walkie talkie radio, "Call off the choppers, we found them."

Anthony and I climbed into the vehicle with the last bit of our remaining energy.

"What's their condition?" The walkie talkie spoke back.

"Dazed and dehydrated, but they're okay."

Sitting in the back of the vehicle, just being *carried* back to the start, was a surreal experience. We had about four miles left to hike, and now we didn't have to take one more step. We just got to ride, in a vehicle.

The woman looked at us in the rearview mirror and said, "We called your emergency contacts. Emilee, we couldn't get ahold of your mother."

"Could you get ahold of mine?" Anthony asked.

"Yes."

"Shit."

"I'd suggest calling her and letting her know that you're okay."

"Why in hell did we put our *mothers* down as emergency contacts? They aren't even in the country. There's nothing that they can do," Anthony said.

I laughed, agreeing with him. But we didn't have any Canadian emergency contacts.

The choppers were just landing as we arrived back to the start where my car was parked. One of the pilots hopped out and ran over to us, looking excited. "You guys found out the hard way that this mountain is impassable. I have thought about climbing it several times before, but when I flew over it with my helicopter, I could see that it cliffed off and you can't get past that section."

We weren't sure what to say. We just smiled a slight smile and nodded our heads.

"Thank you so much for being here," Anthony said. "We were trying to get your attention down here, but that fallen timber was so thick you guys couldn't see us."

"It's all good, I'm glad you both are okay," the pilot said. "Now, go drink a lot of water and call your mothers."

By this point, our water bottles were ready. We finished them in a few minutes. We got into both of our cars and decided to drive to the lakeside. Anthony popped open the back of his car and said, "Coffee or beer? We gotta have one celebration drink."

"Both!"

We cracked open two beers and started boiling water for coffee. My stomach by this point felt like it was eating its own insides. I appreciated the feeling of it. Being completely devoid of food and only quenching my thirst with the refreshing taste of beer and the warming hug of coffee. I am human. I hunger. I thirst. And I, in a weird way, enjoy the feeling of lacking—in order to feel the reward of having.

"I've climbed a lot of mountains," Anthony began, relaxing on the ground with his beer, "but that one was a niner on the gnar-gnar scale. That one was tough."

Anthony had climbed over fifty mountains by this point. Me? One. Old Goat Mountain was it.

I felt like a baby for having panicked, cried, and at one point even begged him to call Search and Rescue the night before so we could be rescued off the mountainside. Rescued. After getting myself into a situation where I was stuck, I wanted to be rescued. Just undo all of the steps before that, erase my part in the plan, and solve it with one chopper ride off that mountainside. But that's not what happened. We weren't saved. We had to save ourselves. It made me think: where else am I desiring to just be saved? For someone to roll up in my life and erase all the steps I'd taken to get to where I was? To undo the emotions I held for myself that I wasn't enough, I would never be enough, and there was something wrong with me because I couldn't commit to a relationship. I reflected on Kim and Avia. How I couldn't speak up to the vacuum she-devil who told me I wouldn't be able to accomplish much in life if I couldn't put the stupid old vacuum together. The fall out of the tree—I was saved. But how, dear God, how could I stand up and save myself?

WHAT DAY IS IT AND HOW DO I SAVE MYSELF?

"You doing alright?" Anthony broke my train of thought.

"Yeah, I was just thinking about life, being stuck on that mountain just made me feel so *human*. I don't know how else to describe it, and makes me think about what's possible."

"Yeah, real shit. I feel you. I think about stuff like that too."

We sat in silence and then Anthony glanced at his watch, and said, "We gotta go call our mothers."

We drove back to the welcome center where we first looked at the maps. I didn't feel like I was in any rush, my momma didn't know anything. But her answer would lead me to believe otherwise.

"There you are!" She gasped, as she answered the phone. "I have been trying to calm myself and tell myself that you're okay, but it has been a really hard day."

I was confused, wondering if maybe she had found out somehow. Did Anthony's mom call my mom?

She continued, "Do you know what day it is?"

Just as she said this, a black screen appeared over the TV in the Banff Welcome Center revealing the day and time. August 20. The exact day I fell out of the tree in Minnesota.

"Holy shit," I said.

"Yeah! It's the day of your accident. I just have been hoping you're doing okay. How's Canada?"

"You have no idea."

I wasn't sure if this was one of those scenarios where "what she doesn't know, won't hurt her" was the way to go, or if the coincidence was just too ironic and I had to share what truly happened. I paused for a while.

"Em, you're not doing okay, are you? I felt something was off. Just had that mother's feeling."

"I have to tell you something."

I told her the entire story: the mountain-prep, the mountain climb, the mountain fail, the freezing, the climbing, the rope getting stuck, the terror, the helicopter, all of it. Helicopters were coming to rescue me, on the same day, five years apart. What an anniversary.

A message came through on my WhatsApp from Mike: "I can't wait to see you!! We will be in Banff tomorrow evening." I saw the message and was quiet once again on the phone with my mother. She wasn't saying much either. When would I stop making such life-threatening decisions? Why couldn't I just sit in a nice apartment somewhere and go to work like a normal person? And then come home and engage in activities like couples bowling and prayer meetings. Drunk tomahawk throwing would be safer than this. Anything would be safer than this.

That night Anthony's mother offered to cover the cost of our stay at an international hostel. A stunning log cabin nestled in the mountainside.

We drove our vehicles up the winding road and were greeted by people of all colors and nations. We unpacked our belongings and brought them inside, setting up in a co-ed dorm. I had never stayed in a hostel before. Our bedroom had eight bunkbeds in it. Downstairs was a great open kitchen space with beautiful stainless-steel appliances and counter-spaces to make our own meals. There were all kinds of delicious things leftover in the fridge labeled "free to use" that included organic oats, almond milk in small containers, beets, goat cheese, and chives. Who leaves these kinds of ingredients behind?

"I gotta go call Mike and tell him what happened," I said to Anthony after we got all our stuff set up.

He nodded, and went to work making dinner—a plate of sliced veggies, sprouts, nuts, and olive oil.

I found the laundry room and called Mike. He wasn't happy with the whole story. I was hopeful that he would think it was a rad story, something amazing had just happened. I felt alive on a whole new level. But he was just worried about my safety, and a little frustrated that I would make such a risky decision.

Two hours later, I emerged from the laundry room, at nine p.m. Anthony was still waiting for me to eat. We cracked open a few beers, and it dawned on me that I can't even enjoy a beer with Mike. He was too young. Just twenty years old, while I was twenty-two. In just one year graduating from college, I could feel myself, now living on my own in a different state, and getting stuck on mountaintops, growing away from who I was and apart from who he is. Anthony and I crawled into our matching top-bunk beds and fell asleep, probably mid-sentence. We were exhausted, our bodies heavy with torn muscles.

Anthony's lifestyle mirrored mine. His wants mirrored mine. We woke up, sipped coffee, and then grabbed our yoga mats and set up facing the big open window overlooking the snowcapped Canadian mountains. Silently, we allowed our bodies to be led by our breath. In a flow of movement like poetry, we worked out the muscle tension and energy trapped in our bodies from panic the day prior. And then, he was off. Onto the next adventure. Watching him drive away, I felt like I had never known someone who understands my soul so well. And now, I was alone. Downtown in Alberta, Canada, I found a little coffee shop to sit and write the story that had just happened. Two lattes down, some French toast, and a call to one of my best friends, Taylor, and her fiancé, Garrett.

They listened, hanging on every word, and couldn't believe how I had just been through that. I laughed, in nervousness; I couldn't believe I had just done that either. Not intentionally. But, how many of the world's greatest things happen *intentionally*?

Banff and The Boyfriend

Mike and his family arrived that evening and I met them in an Airbnb. The location was clean, safe, and monitored by cameras. I put on a pair of blue jeans that were snug on my hips when I moved out to Idaho, but now they wouldn't even stay up. They fell down around my thighs. I pulled them up again, astonished. Have I lost that much weight? I took a piece of paracord, cut it with my father's deer knife, and tied a half hitch knot to make a belt.

Seeing Mike brought a familiar feeling of confused comfort. I hugged him for a long time and told myself that he was home to me. I had made it home. And in a few years, or maybe next summer, we would be married.

Except the next three days that I spent with Mike and his family didn't feel like home. I felt outside of myself and outside of them. I secretly wanted Anthony to come back so we could keep talking about the depth of humanity, the passion in a heart that yearns for risk, and yoga. If I told Mike's family that I did yoga, they would think I was worshipping the devil. A phrase I heard a few times growing up in the Christian church. Yoga was bad. But why, oh why, did it feel so good? And what can be wrong with moving your body?

We enjoyed delicious food, went on a long hike to the top of a peak in Banff (a much safer peak, with bear spray—Anthony and I didn't even *think* of bear spray), and I was included in family pictures. Standing by the Banff National Park sign, there we all were. But I felt, smiling nicely for the photo, that it wouldn't always be this way—me in their family portraits. When the time arrived for his family to leave, I held onto Mike and sobbed. I didn't know why I was crying so much. I knew I didn't feel the way for him that I should if we were going to get married. I knew there was more, but I was afraid to leave this good thing behind. Why couldn't I just make it work? Why did I have to move to another state and change who I was?

They say in the Christian church that the way you drift away from Christianity is a slow fade. There's a song about it by Casting Crowns. *Black and white turn to gray.* I felt myself using all sorts of different colors than just black, white, or gray. I had splashed magenta-orange of the mountain sunrise, lavender night of the Canada sky, iron-red of the Idaho canyons, aqua blue in the high alpine lakes, and all of the brilliant colors woven into all of the international flags hanging in the entranceway to the hostel. The path that was black and white, tux and wedding dress, seemed like the step I was supposed to take. All my other friends were getting married and starting their lives. What was I doing with mine?

Mike and I decided to plan for another trip where we could see each other—Red Rocks, Nevada. A spot just outside of Las Vegas that we both wanted to climb. Then, we said our goodbyes and I was alone. This time, I decided to stay in a campground. The $30 campground. After eating plates of angel hair and bison meatball spaghetti, delicious pastries, and enjoying the three days of luxury with Mike's family, I was alone in the chilly nights again. In a different country. I set up my tent, which was only ten feet away from other tents. We were smashed in on this little plot in the center of Alberta, Canada. I sat in my tent at seven p.m. and made tortilla roll-ups with peanut butter and sliced bananas. I made one, and then another, and then a third. I just kept eating. Maybe if I kept eating, I wouldn't have to think about all of the stress of not knowing where my life was going. Wishing I could have the simple mind to just settle down, get married, and live a normal life. But I wanted experiences like the one Anthony and I shared. Those fed my soul. They brought me to the edge of my existence, just like falling from the tree, to truly see what was possible in the human spirit. The next day, I woke up, packed up my tent, and drove back to Idaho.

The Days Are Long, But the Weeks Are Short

The days are long, but the weeks are short was a phrase the other wilderness guides used for their WildRidge shifts. I found this to be very true as I started my next shift, this time with the wild hares. The group nobody wanted to be in.

Seated at the round table, Brent unfolded a little sheet of paper where he had written down groupings of instructors. It fostered the same anxious anticipation when the teacher in elementary school would declare: "I'll be putting you in pairs this time." Candice, Tucker, and Joan—girls' group. Tom, Anthony, and Steph—boys' group. William, Emilee, and Trent—wild hares.

My heart sank. I am with *William* again? Are you kidding me? He flashed a side-ways smile at me and nodded his head. I felt some sort of comfort in his affirmation of me, but quickly blocked it out and stiffened up straight in my seat with a "can-do" attitude. I nodded back with a tight smile. And then we were back, once again, in an open desert camp surrounded by sandstone canyons and twelve orange dome-shaped tents.

"Let's set up a group to meet all the kids," William said.

The three of us—William, Trent, and I—sat down in a circle of ten students. Two of them still off in their own worlds meandering around camp.

"Will you go get those other two guys?" William asked me.

Walking over to them, I tried to use my most instructor-type voice, "Hey, guys, let's go, we're meeting over here."

One kid was sitting at a picnic table coloring, and glanced up at me like he had no idea the instructors had even swapped out. "Oh, sorry, I'll head over there now."

The other kid, sitting on the ground, facing away from the group, had a stick in his hand and was drawing circles of all different sizes in the sand.

"I don't care," he said. "Have group without me."

"We need the entire group present—what's your name?"

"Devon," he said.

"Will you please come over to join the group, Devon?"

He had long black hair that covered his eyes. Devon's aura was dark, but not in an evil way, more-so in a hurting way. His demeanor was hulled over, like the wind had been knocked out of him and never put back inside of his lungs. Sitting half out of his backpack was a spiral-bound notebook.

"What if you didn't speak in group, and you just wrote down what you have to say?" I asked.

"Sure," Devon said, slowly standing up. His entire energy seemed off, like he might just stumble and fall over with the slightest miss-step.

Devon followed me, and sat closer than normal.

One by one, the students introduced themselves. While the introductions in the girls' group all seemed productive and healing, the wild hares seemed stagnant. They shared their names, where they're from, and what landed them in wilderness therapy.

Most of their responses fell into one of these categories: My parents got divorced and they don't know what to do with me, I was addicted to video games, I hate school, and I don't know why I'm here.

When the circle made it to Devon, he looked at me.

"Devon is going to write his response," I said. "He doesn't want to speak in group today."

Devon opened his notebook and wrote down one sentence. Resisting the urge to lean over and read what he wrote, I smiled and continued on with my introduction. Devon closed his notebook and put it into his backpack.

Wilderness therapy is a lot of groups. Meetings where we sit as low to the ground as possible, sometimes around a campfire and other times on a desert road after one of the kids just had a meltdown. Some of them were blow-ups, others were silent in trailing behind and acting as if their body were just a ghost of a presence.

My favorite groups were at night, around the campfire. Following group that night, Devon revealed to me his second written response for group that day. In an angled sentence to the right corner of the page, he wrote in tiny, messy letters, "I want to die."

Now, before we can be true wilderness therapy guides, we have to do these trainings. One is called "Non-Violent Crisis Intervention" and the other is basic CPR. To be a lead guide, you must have a Wilderness First

Responder training. At the time, I had completed Non-Violent Crisis Intervention Training (NVCI) and CPR. Those trainings can never truly prepare you for the quickness of dealing with these scenarios in real time. In NVCI, we took turns acting the student part and practicing NVCI to de-escalate a scenario. We practiced scenarios where students would run off into the desert, saying that they were going kill themselves, and we'd follow. Scenarios where students come at you with tent stakes or whatever else they can find.

Scenarios you don't actually think you'll be in—until you're in them. And now, that cool damp room where you learned the "procedure" is here and present.

What do I do with a child that wants to die? And I'm in charge of keeping him alive?

Devon's detachment from the group and attachment to me was concerning and also comforting. William, entertainer and carouser of hearts, grew frustrated that Devon wouldn't open up to him.

A few days into our two-week period with the wild hares group, William began to challenge Devon to speak up. He refused. Our days were long and hot, in the hundreds at times. Sandstorms whipped through camp, rattling tents, and destroying shelters. The kids all had a goal of reducing their need for comfort, which, in the desert, looked like relying on the natural elements over the physical.

Each student is set-up with "physical comforts" such as a tent. But as they grow in their ability to rely on themselves emotionally and the desert physically, they begin to build their own shelters using rocks, sticks, and a tarp. We only had one kid at tarp-status. His name was Chris.

Chris was the kid who gave a response something like "I'm just here because my parents got divorced and they don't know what to do with me."

He was calm, cool, and collected. Chris didn't even seem to have resentment towards his parents for placing him in wildness therapy while they figured out their own lives, separately. Kids like him made me more nervous for this thing called "Ignite." Half-way through the kids' wilderness therapy excursions, their parents would come to stay in the desert. They had nicer tents, better food, coffee (the kids *never* got coffee), and extras of whatever they wanted or needed. They were, after all, the pocketbook to keep the programing running. Ignite was where we could see all the connections—from parent to child. The apple truly doesn't fall to far from the tree sometimes. If the student disrespects authority, I bet the father does too. If the student has a very negative mindset and believes nothing works out for them, I bet the mother does too. It was like working with the student, mirrored by two more people that reflect the student—just a more complex version of that child.

Chris had a handwritten calendar in his notebook, and each night he would cross off another day. Fifty-seven days in total. Devon was on day seventeen.

The weeks moved in a cyclical nature, which, took about three months to get used to. Mondays and Wednesdays were therapy days, where a licensed mental health therapist, such as my cousin, Avia, would visit the kids. The kids were only allowed to be alone with the therapist, unless they were at serious risk of hurting themselves or others. In which case, a guide would sit in on the therapy meeting with the child and the counselor.

Tuesdays were for equine therapy where we visited a real cowboy named Curtis and his majestic horses. Curtis was about fifty-seven years old, and was dating people my age. He was currently courting his to-be seventh wife, a young violist with soft blonde hair and gentle, innocent eyes. Curtis and his new love, Alice, could be seen in town playing their instruments together. Curtis played the guitar, and they sang like songbirds together. Harmonizing and looking into each other's eyes, his cowboy boot gently taping the wooden floor from a heel buckled around a barstool he sat on. His energy, I must say, was seductive. When he listened to you speak, he would maintain eye contact the entire time, leaning in and eyes twinkling. His hands were rough from working the field, but the way he instructed the horses was so gentle.

"Go ahead, match up with your horses," Curtis would say to the kids. "They will know when you're the right fit for them; you'll be able to feel that energy. That pull. One of them will choose you, and all you must do is accept their gentle invitation."

His S's were always carried out a bit longer, like the ringing of a bell. Curtis always had an extra big smile when he saw me. He'd nod his head with a dashing smile and say, "There she is, come on in here, I need a hug." He'd step in close and pull my haven't-showered-in-a-week body towards himself in a longer-than-normal embrace. I would just smile and enjoy the moment, knowing Curtis is Curtis.

Thursdays were "base days." We traveled to our abandoned hospital headquarters once a week to re-stock. Lead guides were required to take vitals of all the kids, including blood pressure, temperature, and pulse. They were also required to ensure each of the kids had proper clothing such as socks, boots, and jackets in the wintertime. On Thursdays we'd refill the kids' medications and they would take their once-a-week shower. We too, if we were lucky, got to shower ourselves. Thursdays were good days.

On Fridays we began expeditions—a three-day excursion. Backpacking, snowshoeing, hiking, rock climbing, or some sort of adventure. Expeditions squeezed the ick and the anger from both us and the kids. Most of the breakdowns, and the breakthroughs for that matter, happened on expeditions. It too, was where us as guides bonded. Night after night, under the Idaho-starry sky, we shared our wins, hopes, fears, and even some of our deepest secrets.

Keys to New Beginnings

Following that shift, William had to stay a bit longer with Brent to discuss how the two-week period went. To give feedback about the students, and probably about me as a new guide. Right before I walked out the door, William called to me, "Hey, Em, come here a minute."

I walked back over to him and noticed a key in his hand.

"I'll be home in an hour, but here's my house key. I know you don't have a home right now."

It was true and it wasn't true. I could go back to Avia's house, but there was Kim. And I really didn't want to see Kim anymore. A few of the nights I had just slept in my car somewhere in the mountains. That wasn't exactly ideal either. I took the key, and said, "Thanks, see you in a bit."

The drive was about an hour from headquarters. I called Mike again and told him about Devon, Chris, and the other students. I decided to leave out details about William. Or the fact that I was going to his house to stay for... an unknown period of time.

"What are you going to do now?" Mike asked.

"Just travel around probably and visit places."

When William arrived, I was still on the phone with Mike. I noticed myself trying to end the conversation with Mike, so I could talk to William.

"Well, I'm gonna get some dinner," I said. "I'll talk to you later. I love you."

"I love you too," Mike said.

William dropped his heavy green backpack onto the floor. He peeled his shirt off and threw it into a hamper, and then grabbed a towel and said, "How's the boyfriend?"

"Good, it was nice to talk to him. Gonna shower?"

"Yeah, then some of us are planning to get together for burgers and beers later if you want to join."

"Okay," I said. "Sure."

William turned his head a little, as if he was surprised. "You're really going to come?"

"Yeah," I said.

"Sounded like you already had dinner plans when you were just on the phone."

"Oh, no," I said, beginning to stutter, "I, just, we had been talking for a while and..."

"And you didn't want to tell him you were done talking?"

"Is that weird?"

"No," he said. "We can talk in a bit. I stink."

William stepped into the bathroom and took maybe the longest shower of anyone I'd ever known. As clouds of steam puffed from underneath the door, I looked around his apartment familiarizing myself with all of this stuff. A vinyl record player with folk music artists stacked in a bunch. A futon with a blue blanket from college folded neatly over the top. A fabric wall covering of a tiger that looked like it was tripping on acid.

As soon as he got out, now just wearing a towel, he sat on the futon next to me and pulled out a Hookah.

"Do you smoke?" He asked, gesturing towards me with the Hookah.

"No," I said. "But I don't mind if you do."

He laughed that annoyingly attractive laugh and said, "alright!"

After a few puffs, his body visually relaxed and he laid back on the futon as if I were his shrink and he was in session. I sat cross-legged on the couch, opposite the end from him, and we talked about life. Every single aspect of it. We were late to dinner, and I could feel the shift of eyes like heat carried in the wind from a wildfire, when William and I showed up... together.

We even sat by each other, and laughed about the two-week shift we just finished. Things that weren't really funny, but if we didn't laugh about them, they would remain extremely weighty. Several drinks later, our bills arrived, and William took mine out of my hand and said, "I've got this."

"No, you don't," I said.

"Yes, I want to pay for yours," William said. "You did great this shift, and I am so grateful that I got to be with you."

We returned to his two-bedroom apartment and slept in separate bedrooms. Me, on a blow-up mattress that was from another girl that stayed at the house sometimes. And he slept on his bed. The one he hauled from New York to Dot, Idaho. I thought about my own lack of preparation moving here: all I brought was a basket full of clothes and my backpacking gear. He brought his bed, a TV, floor rugs, and even kitchenware. He seemed to be much more committed to Idaho than myself.

William and I spent almost every day together for the next seventy-five days. We returned to WildRidge and Brent would tell us for the next three shifts that William and I were once again working together. He said we worked so well together. It was now winter, and we were staying with our groups in canvas-domed yurts. The space to move around was very limited, especially with twelve teenage boys. Cots were set up all around the perimeter of the yurt, stacked one on top of the other like bunk beds. As the only female in the group, every morning and night, I changed out of my clothes inside of my sleeping bag—a trick I got to be quite good at. There truly wasn't much to change. The only difference was putting on and removing my sports bra, and changing my pants. I had these fuzzy leggings that I would wear each night. They were like my signal that I had made it—the day was finally over.

The elements in the desert were like amplifiers for emotions. Particles of sand pelted our skin in the summer's wild wind and in the winter? Winter was harsh and internal. We were more lenient with the groups and didn't force as much movement while backpacking. Our groups were transported by vehicles more than our legs. And when we made it to our next yurt destination, we sat inside and worked on paper items. Journaling, workbooks, Sudoku, creative writing, and tic-tac-toe. In my journal, I still wrote about Mike. Saying things like I couldn't wait to return to him, and we will build our life together and worship God. After I'd shut my journal, I'd go sit next to William on his cot and share stories about life back home. The kids asleep, and the flicker of a wood-heated stove lighting our faces. Had Mike and I ever been this close? Sitting next to one another sharing stories about our lives, and wreaking of body odor from not showering for a week?

It started with the innocence of tea. Every night, he would make tea using my mug and we'd share sips. We could cover for each other during the day, and then sit calmly by each other at night and sip tea—laughing and enjoying each other's company. The cot bent more when we both sat on it, pushing our sides together. We grew so close that I decided to take time away from him, in fear that we'd cross lines that one can't cross back over. I went to stay with Avia and decided to plan a surprise trip back to Mike. All of this wilderness therapy had made me question our relationship, and I didn't want to give up. I wanted to fulfill my promise to him.

His birthday was in the spring, and so I decided to fly back to Minnesota. I worked with the director of the rock-climbing wall facility to put up a pre-recorded video of myself wishing him a happy birthday from Idaho. Snowy mountains peaked in the background. The video played one night while he was climbing. Mike paused, and watched my face projected high on the wall: telling him how much I miss him and can't wait to be together again. And then, I came walking out from behind the rock wall. He was shocked, and I was too—because I knew. I knew that soon after this, I would leave. The same line that I didn't want to cross with William was a line that I had stepped away from with Mike. I couldn't bring myself to return to a person whose life still reflected a life I didn't know any longer. It only took eight months, and I had completely shifted into a different longing. A longing to be free from the Midwest mentality of getting married so young. I didn't know that I had a choice. I thought if things were going okay (and they were) then why wouldn't we get married? It was the next step.

But it wasn't the step I wanted. Mike and I spent two days together that were the color of off-white. There was nothing wrong, but it didn't feel right either. I returned to the airport to fly back to Idaho. Sitting in my seat before take-off, a message from William came through: "Let me know when you land! I'll be here waiting for you."

What Does True Love Really Feel Like?

These moments on airplanes have always been defining snapshots for me. The take-off. No matter what city I was leaving or city I was going to, the airplane take-off was a moment of stillness to capture the contour of the land and what it represented for me at that time. Taking off from Minnesota to South Africa was freedom and the pursuit of something greater. Taking off from Idaho to Minnesota was exciting, I was returning to the one that I thought I would marry. I tried to imagine myself in the white dress and the backyard wedding. The scripture readings, and my friends and parents dabbing their teary eyes. And just like that: the takeoff back to Idaho from Minnesota brought tears of transformation. It was time to accept that I no longer fit into the life that I thought I wanted to build. I wasn't the same, and I didn't want to remain the same.

I texted William back: "See you soon! Thanks for being there."

When I got back, William had bought a new vehicle without telling me. His grandpa-old Buick had transformed into a brand-new sporty SUV. He had a water bottle and snacks waiting for me in the center console. He was calm, too calm. I felt swirls of emotion inside, but his demeanor told me he wasn't confused at all.

We made it back to his house and immediately upon walking inside, William said we need to talk about something. I set my bags down on the leaky air mattress and said a quick prayer that went something like this: *Shit-shit-fuck-shit, what now?* I tried to act calm as I re-emerged from the spare bedroom. Would I still be sleeping in there?

Standing in the kitchen with a cup of coffee, he began, "I just want... do you want some coffee?" He asked, pointing towards the Keurig on the counter.

"I'd love some, thanks."

William took out the old pod and replaced it with a new one—

knowing that my favorite was medium roast. As the coffee dripped into the mug, his calm demeanor shifted. He rubbed his hands together and looked at the coffee and then back to me.

"I want to tell you that I really like you," he said. "I don't want to just be friends."

I was surprised he didn't wait for the coffee to finish, he just blurted it out like he had been waiting to say that for the past six months. My heart sank. I didn't want to be with Mike. But did I want to be with William? I didn't know how I felt so I did what any girl does to break the awkward silence—absolutely nothing. I froze, and stared at him.

William half-smiled and laughed his jock-like laugh and said, "This doesn't look so good. You're not responding."

"Yeah, I just don't know what to say, I mean, we're so close as friends and I don't want to lose that," I said. "And besides, I am still in a relationship, I just went home to visit him, remember?"

"Right, and how did that go? Think you're still gonna go back and marry him?"

He was right. William had spent so much time with me, he could see right through me.

"Em, you rarely bring him up. You don't really want to talk to him, but you feel like you should. You're spending all of your time with me, and we have a blast together. What's the issue?"

"The issue is that I am confused by you," I said.

My boundaries were still penitentiary-thick, and I told him that I was still taken.

When we returned to WildRidge for our next shift, I got some harsh news: I wouldn't be going into the field because we were over-staffed. Our numbers had dropped so low over the winter months that they didn't need extra instructors and I still didn't have my WFR (Wilderness First Responder) training. So, I decided to sign up for one and complete the training over the next two weeks, in Sandy, Utah, about thirty minutes south of Salt Lake City.

Me and my little orange car drove over mountainous passes and through dead-zones. I followed a rectangular GPS that hung from my windshield by a suction cup. Sometimes the road that I was driving on wasn't even on the GPS, it just looked like I was driving on some planet with no roads. The "roaming" signal constantly flashing and searching for signal. I arrived late the night before the training and parked along a winding mountainous road. My two-door Cobalt had bucket seats, and wasn't too comfortable for sleeping in. It was fifteen degrees outside, but I decided to hike half a mile up a trail and set up my tent along there. In my pack was a sleeping bag, extra clothes, a small backpacking stove, and a good small-batch-brewed IPA.

My fingers froze as I de-gloved them for a few consecutive minutes to set my tent up, and then put them back on and shivered. On the trail, ice crystals charmed and hardened the imprints of hikers from the day prior. The sound, while walking on them, is like a small version of glaciers breaking to make room for a big ship in the ocean. Crashing open. But these were crashing together, solidifying the imprint of yesterday. And tomorrow, with the sunrise, the trail would turn to mush and change once again—imprinted by a whole new set of boots.

Sitting in my tent, I left the zipper open and facing towards the last sinking moments of the sun. A ball of energy and light, swallowed up by the tree line. Puffs of smoke outlining my every breath showed me it was well below freezing. I put my gloves on and cracked open the beer I had packed. Just me, this beverage, and a sunset. Freezing. My mind wandered to William's group heading out into the field. I felt I had been spared; I didn't want to be stuck with him again. Close together and enjoying each other, but not confronting anything. I wanted it to remain the same. Didn't I? He was right, I never had that much fun with anyone. And it would only get better with my upcoming birthday.

The WFR course in Utah was a week-long course. We spent eight hours a day studying the body, and worse-case scenarios when shit goes wrong in the backcountry. One of the things we had to do was build a device to pull in-line traction on a mock femur break. We used climbing ropes, padding from foldable camp chairs, and a series of learned knots. We practiced this at a cobble-stone outdoor rock wall. I had never climbed on rock like that before. It looked like someone had perfectly placed round rocks in a pattern and poured cement over them. The others in the group were all from the same wilderness therapy program, and therefore, knew each other. Some of them were coupled off, and others were nomads like myself. There was one I became increasingly interested in over the week, as we typically partnered together on the mock injuries. He was tall with dark skin that made me want to ask where he was from. I would daydream that he was from Brazil or someplace I'd never been to, but imagined it to have the most beautiful people. I told him to call me "Emmy." It was comforting, and the name I used to be called in elementary and middle school. It made me enjoy returning to my hometown—where they call me "Emmy."

His name was Jesse, and there was just one problem with Jesse. He was engaged. Jesse was twenty-four years old and I wanted to scream at him, "DON'T GET MARRIED, IT'S A TRAP!" It freaked me out, but Jesse was committed. We would spend all afternoon together laughing, sharing meals, and then at the end he would add something about how amazing his fiancé is. I started talking about Mike that way, and told him I was engaged too. I wondered if he truly felt different for this girl, a feeling I didn't know yet. When she called, he seemed happy. When Mike called, it felt like I was supposed to answer. I was supposed to *feel* a certain way. I was supposed to be something that I just wasn't, or we weren't.

The final day of our WFR training arrived, and we had this big test to take. Jesse and I quizzed each other, and then I grew increasingly anxious for what was happening for Jesse and not happening for me. He noticed I wasn't feeling well, I was shaking. Nervous about the exam, yes, but also nervous about my love life.

"Are you okay?" He asked me, sitting in a wooden desk at my side.

"I think I had too much coffee."

The teacher, a round man with extreme outdoor intelligence, came walking over and said, "This is perfect! Let's figure out what's wrong with Emmy. Gather 'round, students."

My face turned the color of a Roma tomato.

He told Jesse to put a blood-pressure cuff on me, check my eyes, my pulse, and take note of the color of my skin. The rest of the class stood around staring at the numbers that Jesse wrote down of a piece of paper with a broken No.2 pencil.

"What's wrong with me? I said.

"Your heart rate is a little high," Jesse said. "But your eyes look good, and your skin is just a little pale."

The instructor stood up straight and said, "Anxiety, this is what anxiety looks like."

The students nodded, and some of them scribbled notes down on a piece of paper.

I wanted to respond, "Oh! Really? I thought I had rabies."

Waiting for the teacher to grade our exams was even more anxiety producing. I started snacking on trail mix, and then emotional-eating trail mix. Like, maybe two whole cups (baker-size, like the one you'd use for flour, cups) of trail mix. Jesse came in and sat next to me, "How do you think you did?"

"I think I did alright," I said. "Not sure what I'll do if I didn't pass. I need this certification."

"Yeah," he said. "This is my second time taking it."

"What! You failed previously?"

"Yes, just once. I tried to take it four months ago."

The teacher started a painstaking process of calling us in one-by-one to tell us our exam scores. I swear he was leaving Jesse and myself for the absolute last. Playing with our minds.

"Emmy," I heard from the back room. The exam room.

"That's you!" Jesse said. "Good luck!"

I smiled a tight smile and walked slowly into the classroom.

The teacher liked to hold anxious energy as long as possible, so he asked how I thought I did first.

"I think I did okay," I said, trying my best at faking confidence.

He smiled and said, "I'd say you did just fine. You passed."

"Really?? I passed?"

"Yes," he said. "You passed."

I went to pack up my gear, which was a sleeping pad and sleeping bag set up in the corner of someone's office who was out of town. That's where I had slept for the last week. Jesse came walking out of the room with both hands lifted in the air.

"You passed?" I asked.

"Yes! Finally!" he said.

"I've got all my stuff packed up, so I think I'm gonna hit the road," I said.

"A few of us guides are going to have cinnamon rolls at that small café in town if you want to join," Jesse said.

I paused for a moment, thought about it, and then decided it would only fester the wound growing in me for this man. I couldn't tell if I wanted to be with him or just feel however he felt. I wanted a glimpse of what marry-the-person love looked like. I thought that's what Mike and

I had, but now, as I am standing here at the second wilderness therapy program I had come to know in the West, I questioned what I even wanted. These people, the granola type who climb rocks and keep crystals for good energy, were able to unlock something within me that my relationship with Mike just couldn't. It was a different sort of friendship. We were similar. I saw them in me and me in them.

HOLY MATRIMONY OR... NOT?

As soon as I turned at the last stop sign in town onto the mountainous pass that would take me back to Idaho, my mind shifted to William. Maybe he was where I was supposed to be. I didn't know, but I did know one thing—this wasn't fair for Mike. He had to know that something in me had changed, and I couldn't entertain the idea of carrying on our holy matrimony. I drove to Sun Valley and sat in a coffee shop, waiting for Avia to get home. Her days were long days. She met with each of the girls in the girls' group for one-on-one sessions, and then met for an hour on the phone with their parents separately outside of being in the field. All of that took place on different days, but still, they were long days. The coffee shop I visited was a place I didn't know at the time, but would be employed at six months later.

Driving to Avia's house, I repeated to myself, "I am going to break up with Mike, I can do this."

I think I just continued to say that right up until I was on her doorstep, and she continued in the mantra with me.

"Em, if it doesn't feel right for right now, then you are free to make that decision."

"Am I really going to break up with my boyfriend right now?" I said.

"Yes, you are!" Avia cheered. "If it's what you want!" She added.

I called him over Skype (yes, *Skype*, that ancient way of telecommunication), and said my piece. Things had changed, and I couldn't go back to Minnesota. I couldn't fulfill my promise of marrying him that following summer. I had to make this decision for myself—I wanted to be twenty-three and free.

His tears stained my heart, but I knew it was still the right decision.

I returned to Avia's living room and sat there feeling a different sort of lightness. Like I suddenly had no restriction, and I might just float up into the abyss. I had no more excuses to not be with William. To not be with myself. No more reasons to return home to Minnesota. I was making a new home. I just wasn't sure if the new open doorway towards William was the right one, either.

William got out of the field and called me immediately.

"Did you pass your exam?" He asked.

"Yes, I did!"

"Awesome, are you coming here?"

Did he just assume that I was going to go there and visit him? I wasn't sure how much freedom I wanted to explore in my relationship with William, but something about his own expression of freedom was wildly attractive to my restriction. But still, I kept my walls thick and high.

That night, I drove to visit William and stopped at a rest stop. An older man came walking out in the starlight and shouted in my direction,

"You lookin' to sell that?"

"My car?" I asked, into the night air.

He wobbled out under the streetlight and said, "Yeah, that Chevy Cobalt is a collector."

"How's that?"

"They don't make many two-doors like that, I bet I could find someone interested in buying it," he said. "Maybe even myself, I might wanna buy that. What kinda vehicle you lookin' for?"

"A truck," I said.

"I bet I could find someone lookin' to sell they truck and let you know."

I didn't even know I was at the stage that I wanted to purchase a truck, but I guess I was. My treadless tires didn't do so well in the mountains.

A few weeks later, and after one more stint with William at WildRidge in the wild hares group, the guy from the rest stop called me. Sure enough, there was a couple who were driving a 2008 black Ford Ranger from Massachusetts to Oregon. They were looking to sell the Ranger, and could meet me in one hour. We met in the parking lot of my bank. As soon as I saw the small truck with a topper on the back and one bench seat in the front, I knew this was my truck. They sold it to me for

$10,000. I tried to be my most independent, prepared self to talk this man down from $10,000. I made it to $9,800, and thought that I was quite negotiation-savvy.

My bank account, however, was definitely under $1,200. I could not afford to pay this thing outright; I'd have to get a loan. They patiently waited for me in the parking lot as I discussed loan rates to purchase the Ranger at my bank. With the bank's extremely high interest rate and the *possibility*, not approval, of a loan, I told the couple that I'd get the loan between now and when I drove out to Oregon to pick it up. Somehow. William said he'd drive with me, if we picked up some weed along the way. I said okay.

William brought his video games, weed, and stellar taste in music, and we drove. Over passes and under highways. Through farm towns and cities. The couple was moving to Corvallis, Oregon, which, went right through Bend, Oregon. William and I made a trip out of the whole thing. We stopped to visit some friends of mine to go rock climbing for one day. We made it to Bend, Oregon, the evening of February 5th, my birthday. We visited two breweries and William made sure I got free things wherever we went that day. He waited for me as I picked out a new outfit in TJ Maxx. He bought my meals, once again. We laughed and genuinely enjoyed our time together. Nothing was a challenge; everything was easy, and I thought maybe I would be able to keep him. Right here, in this friend zone. So that he would stay forever, and we could have this much fun. Lines had yet to be crossed, and something strong within me feared for when they would. There was no returning after that. We would no longer mesh this easily. That night we had Dairy Queen at midnight, and he booked a room with two queen beds. We slept in them, separately.

I couldn't sleep, maybe because of the beer, burger, and Dairy Queen mixing in my stomach. But also, because I was looking at the Delta App on my phone that showed the flight I had purchased to go rock climbing with Mike. Even though we were broken up, we both still planned to go to Red Rocks.

The next morning, William and I stopped at a little café that had four barstool seats, white walls, a glass case of freshly baked cinnamon rolls dripping with icing, muffins, croissants, and granola-type bars with a little wooden sign that read "gluten free." Natural countertops and thriving plants. Beautiful, young women worked behind the counter wearing tan aprons that hung neatly from their thin waists. *Where was I?* How was everything around here so perfect? I was wearing an oversized flannel, jeans that were too tight for me, and hiking boots. William was wearing his favorite sweatshirt that revealed he was, indeed, an impressive athlete in college. It had a big soccer ball and the words "NCAA Champions" sewn over the soccer ball. So final. There was no reversing those stitches.

We had coffee, cinnamon rolls, and visited the thrift store next door before continuing on our journey. Slightly jolted from the strong coffee we had just consumed at the hipster café; I remember being physically excited to hop back into the car with William. To drive and let him play whatever music he wanted. He played LCD Soundsystem, M83, and other bands whose music I couldn't quite describe. Windows down, just playing music loudly and feeling the purest sense of freedom. Could we just be like this forever? Maybe he doesn't need to come to church with me and what does his weed-smoking hobby do to me, anyway? Nothing. He just gets a little more chill and chattier. I can deal with that.

Then, a funny moment happened. Church. When was the last time I went to church? I couldn't remember. And yet, it was this stake in the ground for me. I wanted a God-centered marriage. Didn't I? What did that look like? What if this is what people search their whole lives for, a partner they can adventure with and introduce you to new things? With only a few hours left until we made it to our destination, I took glances over at William and tried to see him in a different light. Still a friend, but what if he were a lover?

Corvallis is a small, quaint town just fifty miles from the western coastline. My loan still hadn't been accepted, which made me nervous. We stopped at a Wells Fargo in Corvallis and spent two hours figuring out loan details. William was making calls on my behalf and meeting with loan officers. I was on the phone with Jeff, the owner of the black Ranger truck I was going to pick up, and my father, who co-signed on the loan for me.

We were both exhausted from trying to figure out insurance, loan options, and my out-of-state license.

"I feel so bad you're along for all of this," I said, after we left the bank.

"Why? I wouldn't want to be anywhere else."

"There's just so much confusion and I feel like a total mess trying to figure all this stuff out," I said.

"I'm here for you, Em, I want to be here for you. This doesn't bother me at all," he said.

He was there for me. And wanted to be? Just simply wanted to be with me? Even if it was for hours and hours waiting on hold for insurance companies?

This—this moment—this next thought would become the largest, most infuriating monster of pain I would come to know: I am not worthy of this. I am not worthy to have someone love me like William did, he would do just about anything to make my life a little bit easier. To prove that I wasn't worthy, I began to imagine all of the other girls that were "better fit" to receive this sort of support. They had long straight hair and probably smoked weed. They played soccer in high school. They were skinny and had tattoos. They weren't me. It was the description of his high school girlfriend, and so, this became the greatest, most gaping wedge I could place between him and myself. His five-year relationship with a high school sweetheart. I had no idea what that would be like. If I could feel this much love from him in six months? What did she experience in the five years they were together? What does a five-year-long relationship even look like? What does a one-year relationship look like?

The more that William pressed on to impress me with his commitment, the more I created this wedge between us. Like one of those fat-head cardboard cutouts, she was now with us. Her name was Abi. Abigail. Of course, she had a long version and then a short version of her name—just like his. Abigail and William. What were they? Bucking-fucking-ham palace's most beloved couple? It became that way in my mind. And nothing that he could say or do would change my mind. It was set in stone: she was the perfect past lover and I was this new misfit. Someone he thought he wanted, but really didn't.

I started to ask questions about Abigail. She was smart, a varsity soccer-star, and from the "rich" side of town. He thought they would be together forever, but soon after freshmen year of college—she broke up with him out of nowhere. He tried to make it work with her again, but the distance of college and, perhaps, the fresh stocking of "fish in the sea," she decided to move on for good. William was devastated. I didn't know what that felt like, not at that time in my life, anyway.

We picked up my truck, and celebrated in Corvallis. I was the new proud owner of a truck, but now, we needed to drive back to Idaho, separately. He drove my Cobalt and I drove my truck. We still sent music back and forth and passed each other on the highway, laughing. It was like observing a beautiful ice sculpture, in all its delicate intricacies, and yet, knowing that it will one day melt away.

We left Idaho as friends, and came back with a new energy between us. I was growing more and more comfortable with him, and began to crave the way his blue eyes rested on me little bit longer than normal. He would just watch me, as if in awe, of how much he loved me. It didn't require any effort. It just was. We made it back to his place and as he took out the keys to unlock his apartment, I knew things would shift. Things already had. Could we make this thing a forever-thing? Or if not a forever-thing, could we make it "a thing?"

What If "A Thing" Is Not "A Forever-Thing?"

In the most natural way, similar to how he invited me into his home, William invited me into his bed. We laid side by side, feeling the warmth of the other person nearby, but not touching. I wanted to feel what it would feel like; just to be close. I had grown to trust him on a friend-level. What would the next level be like?

I inched closer, till the sides of our twenty-three-year-old bodies breathed in opposite flow like the flora of the ocean against one another.

"Do you want this to be something more, or not?" he asked, moving away to get a good look at me.

I was stunned. I thought he would just let this happen, but he wanted to write up and sign contracts first.

"I like you," I said, looking into his eyes.

"Okay, then we are choosing we'll be together?"

"I think so," I said, scanning the room, as if the answers were on the wall.

I didn't find the answers, but I did notice, the name I feared so deeply, written on a mesh banner he had hung in his bedroom. *Abigail*, with a heart beside it. I packaged that fear deep within me, and the proof that her name being hung on his wall revealed that he was still in love with her. My standards lowered, and I told myself I'd never truly be that important to him, so why does it matter anyhow?

"Yes, let's be together."

One cold hand felt the edge of my t-shirt, and then made its way underneath. Slowly moving along my stomach, and ribcage, soothing the scars on my side from the accident. He wrapped even further, around my side and planted his hand firmly on the middle of my bare back. Pulling my body close to his, he said, "We can't go back after this."

I wanted to say, "I know we can't!" and jump out of his bed and save our friendship. The voices of friends from years gone by surfaced in my mind: *Emilee has a brick wall around her heart, Emilee won't ever let anyone in, Emilee won't find someone because she doesn't go to parties, Emilee doesn't open up to boys.*

Instead, I pulled him closer and allowed my lips to taste his. One touch tingled down my spine, inviting his hand to press harder against me. His tongue met mine and the tips circled making everything else relax. My resistance, my fear, my penitentiary-thick walls, came tumbling down.

Kissing, isn't it the most amazing suction into a different Universe? It's like it takes you to places where everything's okay for a moment. Muscle tension releases. Endorphins encompass your entire being and make you feel completely accepted and nurtured.

We kept kissing and kissing, rolling around, and ended up at the foot of the bed. Clothes began to just be barriers to further places we wanted to explore. To my surprise again, he stopped us.

"Wait," he said, grabbing my hand as it moved between his skin and waistband.

"What?" I said, also taking the pause to breathe.

"You don't want to do that. You said you don't want to have sex before marriage and I'm okay with that. I really respect that," he said.

This removed the magical spark of the moment, but opened up a vulnerable portal into conversation about sex.

"How many people have you had sex with? I asked.

"I don't know," he said, taking a moment to count.

That was awkward, knowing he was thinking about this exact intimate moment with how many other girls?

"Maybe eight," he said.

I was still a virgin, and suddenly felt like my goalie-like approach to purity, wasn't such a great idea. I felt so far behind. And if he had gone down this road eight times before, *why would it be special with me*?

I understand now, six years later, that having sex with more than one person in your life is a really good thing. It can be special multiple times. It can be nothing multiple times. It can be life-awakening and all-out body melting. It can feel like an elevation to the next stage in life or it can feel like taking five steps back and a huge mistake. Sex can be all of those things.

But at the time, I couldn't shake the idea of feeling "less than." I was always going to be less than. Maybe he was dreaming of still being with her? When I asked about their break-up, he said it was "devastating." That phrase got stuck in mind on repeat. "It was devastating." What does devastation from someone not wanting to be with you anymore feel like? I hadn't met anyone that I felt that attached to, besides William now. But at the beginning, it wasn't that intense. It was just a friendship.

A few weeks later, I drove to Red Rocks, Nevada, to climb with Mike. We stayed with his aunt, and I talked to William the entire drive out there. How in the world was he not concerned about this? I left with a simple kiss goodbye and a "good luck." For four days, we looked up routes, ate twice what a human our size should eat, and climbed our little hearts out. His aunt lived in Las Vegas with a hot tub, swimming pool, and a separate camper that Mike and I stayed in. We decided to sleep in separate ends of the camper—I couldn't keep the lines straight with William, but I sure as hell would with Mike. He was a phenomenal climber, and very good at supporting me to lead up routes that were steeper than my typical grade. It was on this trip that I climbed my first 5.12. Typically, I was climbing anywhere from 5.9- 5.10 routes. Mike encouraged me to just try it. It was a severely overhung route that required ballsy moves just to make a clip. I made it the first two clips up the sharp lava rock and couldn't believe I was actually going for a third clip on a 5.12. I called for Mike to "take." Meaning, I might fall.

"I've got you," he said. "Keep going."

Here's the thing with rock climbing: it makes life outside of simple movements stop for a moment. As if you're slowly moving through space, and everything around you are quiet and still. You can hear your heartbeat as your body clings to the side of a cliff face, and it's up to you and your confidence level to get you to the next hold. Mind. Over. Matter. I steadied my breath, wrapped my thumb around my pointer finger, putting pressure on the hold, and stood up. I scanned and scanned and couldn't see the next hold. I threw a hand up over the rock, just to see what would hold, and found a deep pocket. My fingers locked inside of the pocket as I repositioned my feet to regain balance. I was about four feet above my last clip, meaning, if I fell, I would be jerked back to the last clip and probably smack against the wall.

"Holy shit," I said with a wavering voice.

Mike laughed and said, "Keep going!!"

I had to commit. I balanced over on my right toes, with my hand in the pocket hold still, and felt my way up to the next pincher for my left hand. Shaking, I knew I didn't have much time. I desperately searched beneath me for higher footholds. I found one far out right. I sent my leg out long to reach just the tip of my toe. I could see the next shining clip, there was a good hold right next to it. I just needed to make it there. I inched my way up the wall and then, walked my fingers up to maintain balance and reach the next sturdy hold. I got it. My heart beat faster as I focused on clipping, my hands shaking wildly and almost unable to hold the rope attached to my harness.

"I got it!" I said.

"Yeahhhhhh!!"

The next two clips were like climbing a ladder. I made the final clip, and looked out far over the land. Heat rose off the rocks in swirls of steam. As Mike lowered me to the ground, I compared this feeling to my feeling with William. He would never be able to support me like this. And yet, something in me knew I had to move on. I couldn't entertain the idea of being with Mike again. As we sat in the hot tub with a tangerine sky lighting the distant desert, he began to ask questions.

"Why," he asked. "Why won't this work out? I still want you."

The best way to explain this part is not by me, but my most inspired author and one day, friend. I am writing that now, having no idea if we will ever meet. But, Elizabeth Gilbert, the author of *Eat Pray Love,* and many other bestselling books, explains it this way:

"One thing I do know about intimacy is that there are certain natural laws which govern the sexual experience of two people, and that these laws cannot be budged any more than gravity can be negotiated with. To feel physically comfortable with someone else's body is not a decision you can make. It has very little to do with how two people think or act or talk or even look. The mysterious magnet is either there, buried somewhere deep behind the sternum, or it is not. When it isn't there (as I have learned in the past with heartbreaking clarity) you can no more force it to exist than a surgeon can force a patient's body to accept a kidney from the wrong donor."

Just like Gilbert explains, the love that I had for Mike wasn't the love I knew I needed. The intimacy, the lock of the magnetic heart, simply wasn't there. I drove back to Idaho from Las Vegas, saying goodbye to Mike for the last time, with a freedom in listening to whatever was governing how I loved or didn't love.

Nomad. I was a true nomad. Traveling with my sleeping bag and backpacking camp stove, searching for the next adventure, and trying to experience love in the pure state I knew it existed. But there were so many questions. And, with William, the questions got even louder, bolder, stronger, and more challenging, than any questions I had to wrestle with alongside Mike.

All Good Christians Make It Back to Church, at Some Point

Maybe I needed God back in my life? Maybe I was so off-track with this whole love thing because I didn't have a compass. The God of my youth was comforting, clear, and guided me on which way to go. Sitting on William's couch, I cracked open the gold-dipped pages of my Bible once again. The one my parents bought me in college that has my name inscribed on it in cursive letters. All of the answers were surely in there. And, I found a church that was outgoing and lively, smoke machine and electric guitar included. The pastors were a husband-and-wife African missionary duo. There were two service times: nine and eleven a.m. I woke up early, went for a ten-mile bike ride and thought the entire time about if William would attend church with me. We had talked about it before, and he said he would.

I got back from my bike ride and William was sitting in his Marvel-themed pajama pants, shirtless (revealing all of his tattoos, which, I didn't know at that point if they were attractive or super not attractive), and smoking weed. Clouds of smoke puffed from the living room as I re-entered his apartment with my triathlon bicycle. My mind flashed to the stories of women, now in their sixties, wearing orange and saying into the camera with brittle hair and tired eyes, "it was a slow fade, started with weed, and then, before I knew it, we were sharing needles and shooting heroin for twenty years." I definitely didn't want to be that person. I wanted to return to my church roots. Walking into this scene gave me little hope he was going to be attending church with me in twenty-five minutes.

"Are we still going to church?" I said.

"I didn't know for sure if we were going."

"We talked about this last night," I said.

"Well, we weren't sure."

"Alright, whatever," I said, shaking my head and beginning to tear up.

William stepped in front of me and quickly responded, "Woah, woah, woah, if it's really that important to you, it's that important to me. I will come with you to church."

It was ten forty-five a.m. already, and I needed to change. I washed my face off, put on jeans and a loose-fitting t-shirt, and told him I wanted to go alone. Experts say that communication is key, but there is so much subconscious assumption, I've come to learn, in relationships. We assume the way they are is how they'll always be; and if it doesn't change by *tomorrow*, then we're just shit outta luck. But in the same respect, how long would it remain this way? Would I be that sixty-something-year-old woman sitting befuddled on a different couch with the same person still smoking weed and me gettin' up to go worship Jesus? I guess I didn't really want that either. Or maybe, that wouldn't be so bad? Maybe, we could just learn to accept each other for our different lifestyles, and I could be the cool wife that's totally fine with her husband gettin' blazed every day. *It's totally chill, we accept each other for our differences.*

I walked into the church, fog machine already rolling like a lasting aroma, and cried upon entrance. The couple at the door, bless their hearts, tried to comfort me and say that whatever was happening in my life, God was in control. I found my way to a seat and kept crying. I felt comfortable here, in this familiar place of worship and faith, but I still felt so disconnected. I didn't know anyone and, I also felt there really was something to how William described God: "God was outside, God was free, God was never inside the cement walls of a church." It too was Anthony, the head guide on my next WildRidge stint, who taught me that God can be found in more places than church.

It's all fun and games when two people are flirting around, but after you make that decision to be "committed" to each other, jealousy becomes this invisible glue that seeps and fills each and every crevice of insecurities. Both between the two of you, and internally, inside of you. William wasn't nervous about me with any other field guides, until I was placed in a group with Anthony. The free-spirited, organic-oats eating, IPA sipping, rock-climbing Buddhist—Anthony. We were in the boys' group, for my first time ever, and with the worst, most challenging kid in all of WildRidge's history.

William was extra snug on me as we drove out to the desert in the van once again for a new shift. Anthony, sitting in the seat in front of us, seemed like a welcomed space of freedom for me. He exuded patience and peace, like a presence that can be felt just by looking at him. The mounds of snow from the winter gave way to overflowing streams of water throughout the desert. Abundance of one thing and scarcity right next to it. The boys' group was hidden behind these tall vase-like red canyons that grew and grew until they became a part of the land itself and cliffed off a few miles down the way.

The van dipped through a stream that arrives every spring and disappears each fall, tires stuck with rounds of mud. We drove in between two twenty-foot canyons and then, there they were—twelve orange tents. The lead guides swapped gear, including a GPS coordinate locater in an indestructible case, saws and tools for carving bow drill sets, a knife, the kids' medications, a field book containing all of their information, and an old flip phone with the therapists and staff at headquarters numbers.

The guides leaving the field looked dazed and tired. Their words were clear: take special watch of Dillon. Do whatever you can to keep Dillon safe from himself and the group. At fourteen years old, Dillon was young for the boys' group. He weighed about 115 pounds, and stood no taller than five-foot-five. He had beady eyes like a bull shark and very pale skin.

"Dillon, stay with the group, please. I need to talk to Anthony," he said.

"Why? I'm like a Level II or whatever the fuck you people call a high-risk kid, so I'm supposed to stay with you," Dillon said.

"Yeah, but not right now. Go sit down with the rest of the group," the guide said.

"Emilee, can you go with Dillon?" Anthony asked.

My heart dropped and my back began to sweat, this was only minute one of day one. How was I going to keep this wild card safe, when he wasn't complying within the first couple moments?

"Come on, Dillon, let's go."

"No, fuck you new guides. Who even the fuck are you? I've never seen you before," he said, pointing at me.

"I'm Emilee, and you need to come with me."

"This is going to be a fun two weeks," he said.

"That's your choice," I said.

"Is it my fuckin' choice? I woke up at my home in California and two big men were standing over my bed and told me to get up and put clothes on. They took me here, to this hell hole. I hate it here, and I hate all of you people that think you can help people like me."

With most of the kids in wilderness therapy, there was a light to be found. When you truly looked at them, in their eyes, and got to know them on a personal level, there was always light to be found. Dillon was the exception.

THE MORE CONTROL YOU TRY TO TAKE, THE LESS CONTROL YOU HAVE

I genuinely didn't know what do to with Dillon, other than attempt to puff myself up to appear bolder, bigger, and stronger than I was. If I failed to calm Dillon, then I failed as a guide. I needed to make him calm down, somehow. His tent was set up tight to the head guide's tent. Dillon had to be wrapped in a tarp inside of his sleeping bag inside of his tent, with the entrance facing Anthony's, so that he could hear if/when Dillon tried to run away again. He had attempted to run away three times already.

With love and compassion, Em. That's how I'd treat this scenario, with love and compassion. I would listen to him and maybe he would calm down. Within the first few nights, I quickly understood why the last guides looked so worn out. They probably didn't sleep, just as I wasn't. I'd lay awake at night, listening for movement in Dillon's tent. We thought we were doing a pretty good job, keeping him in sight and somewhat compliant, until day four. Tent check-ins. We didn't have to do this with all the groups, but we did with this one.

Anthony and I took turns checking tents—looking for sharp or harmful items. We also skimmed through their journals looking for any ideas of harming themselves or others. Dillon was sitting in his tent, and refusing to get out.

"Let's not make this more difficult than it has to be," I said, already tired of this shift.

"I got nothin' in here," he said, laughing.

He shifted in his tent, and I could hear liquid splash inside some sort of canister. And the smell. What was that smell? It was poignant and strong.

"What is in your backpack?" I asked.

"Nothing."

"Will you show me? I believe there isn't anything harmful in there, but I just need to see."

He pulled his busted backpack towards the tent's opening and I could see the corner of a gas can.

"Is that a gas can?"

We kept extra gas cans in the storage, where only guides were supposed to go. How he got in there, I have no idea. But he had, and was sniffing gasoline.

I asked him for it, not sure what else to do. Was I supposed to dive in there and tackle him to remove it? Just ask for it? I didn't really believe that he would give it to me, but he did. His hands shaking, he began to tear up and handed the gas can to me.

"Thank you for giving this to me," I said.

"Please don't tell anyone that I stole that!"

"Why did you take it?"

"Because I can't find any other drugs out here. I'm a druggie. What am I supposed to do?"

He got more paranoid as our conversation went on, and I said I didn't need to tell the other guides, but I would have to tell Anthony.

"Just don't take it again, okay?" I said.

"Okay."

Feeling like we had reached a new level of respect and understanding, I walked away with the gas can and a little more confidence. However, the snickering laugh behind me quickly tossed me outside of my moment of calmness. Turning around, Dillon was sitting in his open tent, smiling with unmoved eyes, watching me walk away. Chills ran down my entire body, and I no longer felt safe. With ten days left in the field, my mind and body went into pure operation mode. Don't feel, just operate. Just do the tasks that need to get done each day and ensure my two parts of rest assured sanity: waking up at five fifteen in the morning to boil water and make coffee before the kids woke up, and talking with Anthony at night after the kids went to bed at ten p.m. to laugh off the outrageousness off the day.

There were a lot of hours between five fifteen a.m. and ten p.m.

I had a watch that I'd look at periodically. It felt like time was moving slower. When Dillon had already decided to up and wander away from the group twice, throw rocks at other students, and tear up his journal by eight a.m. By two in the afternoon, he had threatened suicide and pushed Anthony away from him. And by four p.m., he had left the group twice more, explained in detail how to make meth, and seemed like he was enjoying the process of making the entire group miserable.

The part of the day that I dreaded the most was morning call-ins to headquarters. Every morning, promptly at ten a.m., the head guide had to leave the group and do call-ins to headquarters on a two-way radio. This meant I was alone with the entire group. Besides the rage of Dillon, was also eleven other boys who had landed themselves in wilderness therapy for one reason or another. Dillon, sensing fear like a wild animal, enjoyed the torture of the moment. He would just walk out of sight so I couldn't see where he was. I would ask him to come back, and he would be silent—pretending and acting like he was gone. Great hide and seek player. The silent torture would continue until I walked over to find him, at which point, he would double over in laugher.

"What's your problem, kid?" One of the other boys in the group spoke up.

His name was Sam. A tall, quiet, and very smart kid whose father was abusive and his mother simply didn't know what to do with him during the divorce. I must say here that I do not condone wilderness therapy for kids whose parents are going through divorce. But, in this circumstance, Sam was the most stable of the all the boys and I was extremely grateful for his understanding of the moment.

Dillon came back around from behind the rock and said, "What's wrong with me? You fuck-up. At least my parents didn't send me here because they don't know what to do with me."

Sam weighed about 160 pounds, next to Dillon's sopping wet 115. I kind of wanted to sit down in my foldable camp chair, sip my coffee, and watch the show.

"None of us want to be here, but we can't change that," Sam said. "You're making this way worse than it has to be by acting out all the time. I'm tired of your shit. Just listen to Emilee, she's the guide."

It was like a dove had descended and granted me a free pass.

Dillon came back to the group, sat down, and began drawing circles in the sand with a stick. Sam went back to journaling. And then Anthony came walking back from check-in with headquarters. A sigh of relief.

"I've got news!" Anthony said, all excited. "We are going to Fox Burrow this weekend!"

Fox Burrow was a remote spot about forty miles away from our current camp, that was a coveted spot for backpacking. We would pack all the water, food, and supplies we needed for the four days we'd be out there. Miles and miles of desert landscape gave way to a cut in the land that dipped into a shallow riverbed. Life in the form of trees, plants, and shrubs, sprung alongside the river's edge and provided little flatland spots to get out of the sun, near a water source, and camp.

Anthony walked by me and handed me a folded note.

"This is from William," he said.

I was confused at how he got this magical note.

"Did you see him or something?"

One of the scouts was out dropping things off for the wild hares group, William asked if they'd deliver it to you.

"Oh, thank you," I said.

I could barely keep it together how excited I was to read this note. It had its own vibration in my hand, just waiting to be opened and poured out. So, I took an opportunity to seek some alone time in the only place that's possible: the outhouse.

Outhouses don't exactly have the best aroma or ambiance, but I needed to read the note right now. I unfolded it with shaking hands and read all about his wishing he could be with me. Wishing he could be there with this challenging kid to help me. Wishing he could be there to support me. And wishing he could just hold me.

There was nothing I desired more than to just be held, by him. It ached somewhere deep in my soul. I kept the note in my pocket for the rest of the shift, which, was six more days. We all packed up and planned our three-day journey to Fox Burrow.

Dillon sat in the middle seat of the van next to me. Each of the kids set up their tents, with Dillon's facing Anthony's once again. Food in the field was a coveted thing, because if you ran out of something—it was gone until you made it back to base to re-stock. The top items were granola, trail mix, and summer sausage. The kids would manage most of the meals, but sometimes a few items would go missing. In the boys' group, it was the summer sausage that was always of highest desire. We had two packages of it when we left camp, and now, as we opened up the bins to make lunch, they were gone.

This called for a full-on tent and backpack check.

Sam walked by and whispered, "Just check Dillon's tent, I saw him take it."

Anthony and I both knew this was likely the case, but we didn't want to accuse him without checking everyone else's. With lunch on hold, and the heat intensifying under the desert sun, we made each of the kids show us their pair of boots, pair of sandals, socks, one pair of pants, one pair of pajamas, underwear, journal, backpack, utensils for eating, and outer layers.

Dillon was missing his boots, and refused to show us what was in his tent. I walked around the back, and hidden underneath his tent, were the two packages of summer sausage and three oranges. He had cut a hole in the side of his tent, and dropped his boots along the path. An escape route this early in the trip.

With anger rising from the other boys, we decided to have a group.

We circled up and each of them expressed how they were feeling in that moment. Dillon refused to apologize, and said that they were all taking too much of the summer sausage. It took over an hour to come to some sort of agreement, more so, just to get us back to making lunch again at three in the afternoon, and move on with our day of activities.

A few days crept by, like kneeling and crawling through the desert, parched and hoping, just hoping, there would be water on the horizon.

On day three, we decided to go for a longer hike to the canyons in the distance. Dillon requested a "group." Dillon never requests group.

"I want to circle up to say something to the entire group," Dillon said.

Anthony, appearing shocked, went along with it.

"Alright, man, awesome, let's group up," he said.

The rest of the group slowly walked over, not as convinced that this would be an effective group.

He stood there in silence, enjoying the wait. The wait we had on him the entire time. I was tired of waiting, just to see what Dillon would do.

"I want to apologize to Emilee," he said, looking at me. "I've been really disrespectful towards you and it's probably just because you're a woman. Sometimes I can be mean to my mom too and I know I shouldn't be like that so, in front of everyone here, I want to say I'm sorry."

Anthony looked very pleased; I wasn't so convinced this was an honest apology.

"Thank you for saying that," I said. "And I hope you have learned how not to treat women, and see some changes in your behavior."

"Yes, I have."

"Alright!" Anthony said. "That was great! Thanks, Dillon, for sharing that. Let's hike!"

"Can I just hike behind the group... with Emilee?" Dillon asked.

What the fuck in fuck? No, I don't want to hike behind the rest of the group alone with this kid, even if he just put on a show of an apology.

Anthony was on board for it. He, and the rest of the eleven boys, hiked ahead.

I tried to ask him things about life back home, things he likes to do... anything to try to crack the code to this kid. As we walked, and the group got increasingly further and further ahead, I had an urge to yell to Anthony not to get too far away. They kept hiking and hiking, and soon, he was out of ear shot. I was alone.

Dillon's hands were shaking, and I noticed a string tied around his middle finger. He grabbed a note out of his pocket and handed it to me.

With lifeless, dark eyes, he looked at me and said, "This is up to you now."

"What is up to me?" I said.

"He handed me the note and in big letters it said on the top "Tell mom I'm sorry."

The rest of the note read "I found a stray bullet that was active on the ground and made a trigger, which is attached to my finger. As soon as I pull this trigger, my head is going to explode as the bullet that's attached to my head is going to go off. You can watch it happen or move out of the way."

He began to walk off into the sage brush desert yelling and laughing, "It's over now, it's fucking over!"

I froze. Yelled for Anthony. But, nothing. I followed him out to the desert attempting to say he can't do this. I thought for a moment there's no way he knows how to do that, but he also explained in great detail how to make meth (twice) and that process didn't sound easy either. The kid wasn't dumb, he was actually highly intelligent.

"ANTHONY!!" I yelled again and again, until the last kid in the group heard and notified him ahead.

He came running back, and Dillon went running in the opposite direction.

What do I do now?

The rest of the group circled up, while we were dealing with Dillon. Anthony yelled to me, "Stay with the group! I'll go with him."

Dillon stopped running and fell down to the ground crying. Sobbing. Waves of pain and anger releasing from his small frame into the particles of hot sand beneath him.

The rest of the group and I sat in a circle and stared.

Two hours later, a therapist and a few support staff made it out to the field. The therapist met with Anthony and Dillon, now just sitting in the sand. There was a rancher named Rick who would sometimes come out and help with the group transfers. He had also chased kids down on four-wheelers in his younger days. He was no novice to working with kids in wilderness therapy. Rick pulled up next to us in a fourteen-passenger van, and called me over.

"How you doing after that?" he said.

"I'm pretty shook up," I said.

"Yeah, it ain't an easy thing to deal with, but it's part of the job," he said. "You think you're cut out to deal with stuff like this?"

Why is he asking me this right now? Of course, I don't feel cut out to handle suicidal scenarios, does anyone feel ready to handle that?

"I don't know," I said, glancing in his direction.

"Well, ya better figure it out b'cause kids do things like this here."

I thought I was going to get a hug, a sucker, and a teddy bear from this support staff. Not a stern talking to about if I was cut out to be a guide or not. The truth was, I didn't feel like I was. Or maybe I was just getting to the point of being "burned out." At that point, I had been there for over a year.

The Body and Mind Will Do What It Takes to Be Heard by You

After about the eighth day on wilderness trips at WildRidge, I noticed myself detaching from reality. A sort of numbing to get through the remainder of the shift. Anthony and I were quiet during the ride out of the desert away from the boys' group. It was the best and the worst group I'd ever had. It seems that good and bad aren't on a linear plane, it's more on a big circle. Good is right next to bad. Happiness, right next to anger. And love, next to hate. Just like watercolors on a canvas, they can slip so easily, from one into the other—making a whole new shade that's unrecognizable as either. That's kind of how William and I shifted—from friends to lovers to constant arguers. Love to hate. Happiness to anger. The bleeding color of confusion.

We tried to live our lives in parallel form. I went to church and rock climbing with friends, he would come along, but I knew it wasn't his true self. There were changes happening within me, again. I knew that I wasn't going to last at WildRidge much longer. I had since moved into a couple's studio space in their garage near Avia's house in Sun Valley. It had a lofted bed, full kitchen, and a large open living room space. The couple who owned the space, Sune and Vicky, were my first experience of what a truly adventurous couple could look like. They met at an outdoor guiding company, had summited mountains together, and now were living out their adult lives with respect to the risky adventures of their youth. Their library was full of mountaineering books and old relics from climbing partners. Vicky was one of the highest esteemed trauma therapists in area, and Sune was a living legend of outdoor guiding. He had worked with a local private school to build their outdoor program. Sune did everything with compassion and without force. The Universe seemed to provide for him, along with his ability to rest in its embrace and trust its plan. I've never met someone, besides Anthony, who exuded so much love and compassion through just looking into their eyes.

They were gracious enough to accept me, and, at times, William, into the space. Vicky wasn't any sweet ol' Betty. She spoke how she felt. No coatings of sugar, not even the zero-calorie kind. She advised me to figure out what I want and give *zero fucks* about anything or anyone else. She had been in serious relationships before Sune, and cut them off mid-backpacking trip because she knew they weren't right. It didn't seem that easy for me. What was supposed to feel right? William and I talked very seriously about getting married, about creating a life together, and leaving WildRidge. He was just as burned out as myself, but, for some reason, he was still committed. I felt the desire to stay drain a little more from me with each passing shift. His seemed to get stronger.

Just five days into our time off, we got word from other instructors that Dillon had escaped in the middle of the night. He packaged food in his backpack and was found wandering the streets of Dot, about ten miles away. WildRidge called in extra support and transported him to another facility. He was gone.

I felt relieved. But at the same time, I felt like all the work we had put into him was wasted. Where was he going now? Would they just put him on more medication? Keep him in a lockdown facility? I could see, past all of the hurt, terror, and hatred, that he didn't want to be that way. Nobody wants to act that way. People act out when they aren't being heard. When they don't feel seen. Most of the kids that I had worked with, the worst behaving ones anyway, had things happen to them that weren't their fault. Sexual trauma. Family issues. Mental health disorders. They were on the road to figuring out how to deal with it. I guess I was trying to figure the same thing out, and I didn't have any answers. I started listening to podcasts and reading books about the brain and releasing traumas. Nobody comes into this life understanding how to do that. We just feel emotions—like anger. And under it? Is a hurt. But sometimes you have to get through a lot of layers of anger before the tender bed of hurt reveals itself.

To keep myself moving forward, I returned to running. This time, I wanted to see what it would be like to challenge my body in the mountains. I signed up for a 35k in Tillamook, Oregon. William said he would sign up to run it with me. It summited two mountains: Elks and Kings. In the six weeks between me signing up for the race and the start line, I left WildRidge. Both of us were burned out, and so too was my cousin, Avia, the wilderness therapy therapist. She left the week before me, on the account of lack of care for us—the instructors.

She left. I left. But William, he saw opportunity to grow with WildRidge. He stayed.

The Elk and Kings 35k race took place on a Saturday in early October. I had prepared for the race, and felt ready to run it, but William I knew hadn't done anything to train. Three days before the race, William took on one extra week at WildRidge to cover for another instructor. I was headed out there alone.

I planned to sleep in the bed of my truck, which was covered by a raised topper. I put blankets, pillows, sleeping bags, food, water, and my running gear in the back. The drive from Sun Valley, Idaho, to Tillamook, Oregon, was just over ten hours. As soon as I pulled out of Sune and Vicky's driveway, I rolled down my manual windows, and played my music loud, which was a selection of instrumental yoga beats, Taylor Swift, Bone Thugs-n-Harmony, Purity Ring, 2Pac, and The Eagles. *Nothing* in my life is uniform, not even my music selection. This was home to me—my truck and I on an open setting-sun highway. Instead of sadness that William wasn't joining me, there was relief. I wanted to do this by myself. I wanted to prove to myself that even if I can't rely on others, even if we make plans and they fail, I still have myself to pick me back up. I lost service around halfway and decided to pull into a rest stop to climb into the back of my truck and sleep for the night. Tomorrow, I'd finish the drive, and the day after that was the race. The rest stop I pulled into had an outhouse and no other vehicles—good, I'm safe.

I climbed into the back of my truck and stared at the stars through the clear sections in my topper. They flickered bright and the moon's fullness was the only nightlight. I was drifting off to sleep when large headlights pulling into the rest stop frightened me awake. Shit, another vehicle. A trucker. My topper was broken and had no lock, and here I was in the middle of nowhere Oregon with no service. I pulled my backpack close to my chest and grabbed a knife out of the side pocket. A man hopped out of the truck and walked to the outhouse. I wondered if I should quickly jump out, start my truck, and act like I'm leaving. He left the outhouse and noticed my truck. Did he notice me in my truck or just the truck? I couldn't tell. He stopped and stared at my truck—or me—or both. My palms were sweaty holding the knife and I told myself, *I can do this, if I have to, I can do this.*

The man took a few steps towards my truck and then stopped. He stared straight at me, or was he just starting at my truck? I couldn't tell if he could see me or not. What was going through his mind? I'm sure he knew that I didn't have any service, as he probably didn't either. He put his hands in his pockets and then turned around—back towards his truck. I let out a sigh of relief, and hoped he would pack up and leave. He decided to stay there, too. I realized maybe I could be safer with this random trucker man. Maybe it was okay that he was there, and wasn't going to harm me. I dozed off, and then awoke in panic, scanning the rest stop and expecting to see some man standing outside my truck staring in at me. He must have been sleeping in his own truck. Two strangers on the side of a highway.

In the early morning light, I packed up before the trucker and continued on my journey. I didn't drive long, just far enough to stop and sip some coffee. I found a spot in the Mt. Hood National Forest, next to moss-covered trees and manicured trails leading to log bridges over calm streams. I hiked about a mile in, with my French press, JetBoil, Nalgene water bottle, and Organic Fair-Trade coffee. I set up next to the stream, still foggy from the cool of the night, and the haze of the morning. I sat on the ground, cross-legged, and poured myself a steaming hot cup of black coffee into a makeshift mug (which was the cover for my JetBoil). It was a trick I had learned in wilderness therapy to pack less gear. Here I was, in the middle of nowhere, but completely found. Completely at home with myself and the forest. How could I take this breath of freedom and knit it into the fabric of my life? Into my relationships? I didn't know how to share an environment with another, and yet remain myself. I didn't want to blend into my surroundings anymore. In the forest, the stream was powerful and quiet, moving slowly with intention and smoothing out the sharp corners of rocks broken off from boulders up-stream. The trees were a statement. Tall and not without blemish, but rooted deep into the earth's soil, and life-giving. Trees don't hide behind their flaws, they grew with them, stretching out the knots and holes that sometimes make another animal's home. They don't hide their aged skins, they're proud of their extra rings and old man's beard hanging off their brittle limbs. The fertile soil underneath. It accepted what was planted. It nourished what was given to it. And here I was, in harmony, with all of it. I need not act like the stream, the tree, nor the soil beneath, they allowed me to share their space. I was them and they were me. How could I feel that way in a home? With another person?

Leaving the Mt. Hood National Forest, I could feel the strings between William and me being severed one by one. I began to cry just as I made it my truck, climbed in, and said, *"Here we go, baby girl. Let's do this thing."* I arrived at the Tillamook National Forest around four o'clock in the afternoon and went to find a campsite near the start line. An F-150 truck with an extra-large camper pulled in on the opposite side of the dirt road leading to the campsites. It was right next to the river, and had plenty of space. I thought this big-ass truck was going to tell me that since I'm smaller, I gotta leave. A bald white man with heavily freckled skin of about sixty years old rolled down the window and said, "This is the best campsite in the whole campground."

"Oh, you need the space, I can let you have it," I said. "It's just me and my truck right now."

"How about we share it?" he said.

I took about three seconds to think about it and happily responded, "That would be great!"

His wife, an Asian woman, hopped out of the truck soon after they pulled in and asked if anyone else would be joining me.

"Yes," I said. "My husband."

My husband? What? Why did I just say that?

"Oh, very well. Do you know when he will be arriving?" The woman asked.

"Not until later this evening," I said.

"Okay, well, if you need anything before he gets here, let us know. We have a nice shelter, showers, bathroom, and everything in that camper."

"Yeah, it looks really nice!" I said. "Thank you, I'm going into Tillamook to do some scouting and prepare for a race I'm running tomorrow."

"You're running that crazy race in the mountains?" She asked.

I laughed. "Yes," I said. "That's me."

As she walked away, I wanted to yell after her: *What was it like? Did you know he was "The One" for you when you met? William isn't my husband! I was just trying it out!*

I was just trying it out. Just to see what it would feel like to be fully committed to him. To another person. As soon as I said it, my heart sank, and I had my answer. I left the campsite, in tears. The town of Tillamook was just ten minutes away from the campground. I drove up and down the coast, watching the waves crash against big sharp rocks. Not even the crashing cyclical nature of waves can sand down these boulders, I thought. It didn't seem right. How could the trickle, the slow and steady trickle, of a stream, be the better of the two? It took time. A lot of time, consistent repetition, without force, to soothe the rocks lying at the bottom of the iron-red riverbed. And here all of the magnetic energy of the earth's rotation was crashing against these rocks, and only making them more jagged, rough, and unforgiving.

Our runner packets were available for pick-up at the Tillamook Welcome Center. I grabbed my bib, shirt, and information on the trails, aid stations, and start times. The map was a little intimidating. I had never run a race in the mountains before. Elevation gain was something I'd never trained for before this race. Heading back to the campground, the sun was setting, and I made dinner over an open fire. With my night's cup of tea, I climbed back into the back of my truck and left the top portion open. I felt alone and yet so solid in me. Solid in my choices to be here, to challenge my body, and be in new territory. I saw the camper door to the couple sharing the campsite open and the Asian woman came walking out with a Coleman lantern.

I was trying to read my book, *The Way of the Peaceful Warrior* by Dan Millman, with a headlamp around my forehead. It worked, but didn't give off much light. The woman walked to the back of my truck and said, "Hi, I wanted to bring you this lantern," she said. "I thought it would help you see."

She didn't ask about my husband. She didn't ask why I was here alone. She just gave me the lantern. And it did help me see, helped me see a lot more than just the pages of my book.

Freedom from circumstances, I believe, comes first internally. Before you have the facts in front of you. Before your circumstance changes. Before you leave, before it all happens. I turned off my headlamp, closed my book, and laid down in the bed of my truck—with warm tears rolling down the sides of my cheeks. I knew what I was supposed to do, I just didn't want to do it. I prayed to God to help me be free from myself. Help me with the chains I've put on myself. Help me with the prison I've trapped myself in.

"So, You Think You've Signed Up for the Easier Race"

It's seven a.m., and I'm running in place to keep warm before the start of the Elk and Kings 35k. The race director informed us that the 50k, which we all probably wanted to sign up for, but felt like it was a little too much, was actually the easier one. The 35k had much more elevation gain than the 50k. The 50k, he explained, was a nice stretched out course, whereas the 35k was kinda straight up and straight down, and then straight up and straight down again. But, he promised, there would be Crown Royal whisky shots at the top of the second mountain—Kings.

At the sound of the beginning blow horn, I set off fast towards the winding trail that led towards Elk Mountain. Jagged rocks made a steep pathway up the side of the mountain. There was no subtle weaving up the mountain. By the summit of the first peak, my thighs felt like they had chards of glass in-between the muscle fibers. I really didn't know if I would be able to finish the second peak. The steep down climb from the backside of Elk Mountain required a rope tied to a tree at the top of the peak.

Runners took turns holding the rope and walking their feet down the rocky, fifteen-foot section to a spot where the rocky trail continued down, down, down, only to go back up, up, up. I stopped at an aide station between the two mountains and ate a Dixie cup filled with peanut M&M's. And then I had another, and another. I finished that treat off with some crispy bacon and a pickle. I wanted to take my runner's bib off and stand behind the table for the rest of the race just serving other runners and eating more bacon.

"How's the course?" the volunteer behind the table asked.

"It's beautiful," I said. "But, man, it's hard."

"That's good, yeah!" He said, with a big smile, nodding his head.

I wanted to punch him.

"Yeah! It's really good," I said. "Do you think I'll finish by the cut-off time?"

He looked at his watch and said, "You're three hours ahead of the cut-off time. At this point, you would have to get lost, hurt, or actually try to not make the cut-off time."

"I could do one of those things," I said, squatting down low to the ground.

"Oh, come on," he said. "This is what life is all about, meeting the edge of pain and pushing past it. Can you imagine what's on the other side of that?"

And then he took his hands and fanned them out in sky, as if he were magically making a painting appear, and repeated the phrase, "Just imagine!"

With that, I decided to keep chuggin' along. Step by step. A beautiful elf-like man came tiptoeing around the course and looked like he could keep running from here to Kansas. I quickly followed in his wake, hoping I could channel the energy he had. It worked, for a while. I matched my stride with his stride. He tiptoed, I tiptoed. He inhaled, I inhaled. His arms pumped slow and low. I did the same.

I trailed with him until the middle of the next mountain—Kings. And then, I hiked. I could no longer push my body to keep up a pace of running. I was now just hiking, or huffing, up this thing. My legs had never been in so much pain before, and I wondered if I should go sit in an icy stream after the race. And then I remembered something about beer. They would have beer at the end of the race! That became my sole encouragement to finish this thing. Just like the race director promised, at the top of the second mountain, there were men dressed in Kings' attire with crowns and pleated robes. They served slurps of Crown Royal from a community CamelBak pack. Speakers playing the "Game of Thrones" theme song were hidden behind the rocks and trees at the summit. I let my legs move on autopilot to the end of the race. Just barely rolling through.

At the finish line, I watched couples hug, kids surround their parents, and friends high fiving. I found the nearest chair and collapsed into it. Alone. I didn't need someone to celebrate the completion of this difficult race with me, but I longed to be like one of those smiling beautiful girls with their cute boyfriends, or husbands, whatever they were. I felt so on the outside. I found my celebratory glass and got my first round of beer. I sat on the back porch of the Tillamook Welcome Center, where the race ended, and smiled. Even in the pain of confusion, in the face of making hard decisions, I felt so alive. The man behind the aide station was right.

I enjoyed a few beers, ate a sandwich, and returned to my truck. Running the 35k stood in place for me as the shift I needed to make a decision. Our hearts always know what's right, but our minds like to fight for logic and what we see instead of what we feel. Driving back to Idaho, on an open road with the setting sun, I knew what I needed to do. The question was: could I follow through?

How Do I Get the Cheat Codes to Life?

It felt like there was this well of answers somewhere that everyone else could find, but I, for some reason, couldn't find them. The only thing I absolutely knew was that I wanted to be a writer. All else was up in the air. I began pitching magazine articles to *Sun Valley Magazine, Boise Territory*, and started writing a regular column in a local newspaper. I wanted answers—but where would I find them? I went back to church. The pastor spoke about leaving things behind that we know are not for us. In a flowy blue dress, I sat in the middle of the church rows and cried. And cried. I didn't even try to make it a quiet cry. Snot and tears ran down by face. A lady stood up and walked over to me and gave me her own travel tissues. Not like one tissue, the *entire* thing.

I knew this relationship was not for me. I had my whole awakening during my 35k schlep through the Tillamook State Forest. My soul knew its decision, I just had to follow through on it. Still together, but dangling by a cord, I asked if William would meet me at a reservoir. A glistening reservoir with one inconspicuous dirt road that goes for miles and miles back to the black cement highway. I got there before him and wrestled with myself. Maybe we just make out here and make it all better? Maybe this is just a transition for us? Maybe we shouldn't break up? I got out and laid on the hood of my truck—under an intense Idaho sun warming up to temperatures in the nineties by mid-morning. William arrived. We hugged. And decided to drive towards the reservoir. Both of our windows down, dirt kicking up behind both vehicles and disappearing into a smoky mist.

The desert is full of sagebrush. The hippy-kind that healers purchase in other parts of the country to burn and clear the energies in the air. It's everywhere. On some wilderness trips, I would cup my hands on either side of a sagebrush branch, rub them together, and then bring my hands in front of my face like a washing or re-birth and breathe deeply. This entire experience was a clearing—a moment in time where space is made for something new. I just didn't know what the new thing would be and how would I move on from this one? *What if I never find someone who loves me as much as he does?*

We made it to the reservoir, and while I had a whole speech prepared in my mind, I couldn't bring myself to recite any of it. I just stood there, looked him in the eyes, and cried—painful long tears.

"It's okay, Em," he said.

"It isn't okay," I cried through a screen of tears.

"This isn't working for you," he said. "And that's okay."

More uncontrollable sobs.

This was my moment to really end things. To really be done. I didn't even have to say it, he already knew it.

"You're right," I finally said. "But maybe we can work it out somehow? I love you so much."

"We've tried to work this out," he said. "And it isn't working."

He was right. So, we ended things right then and there. *Why couldn't I make any of these relationships work?* What was wrong with me? The thought of him moving on crushed me to my core, but I couldn't keep him—so I had to let him go.

Crying became a normal part of my day, like a daily checklist. Wake up, make the bed, cry, brush teeth while crying, make coffee, cry into that coffee, do some yoga, watch droplets of tears hit the yoga mat like early spring rain, sit in silence, go for a walk, go the grocery store, and then hide my face in the bakery aisle while crying more tears. Visit friends and cry with those friends.

It went on like that for some time until I decided that I needed actual professional help. I was trapped in an obsession with him moving on before me. I knew it would happen. He probably already had? I thought, I need a complete reinvention of myself—maybe I need to move? I decided to call a woman in Washington whom I refer to as my "Asian Mom." We met just months before William and I parted at the City of Rocks in Idaho. We happened to be climbing sections next to each other and she commented on my climbing. I told her I hope to visit Washington soon, and she yelled to me while we were about thirty feet in the air, "Please! Come stay with me! I just divorced my husband of thirty years and moved there by myself. I'm a nurse. I have a two-bedroom condo."

Well, if this wasn't the perfect time to visit my Asian Mom, I didn't know what would be. I drove to Tacoma, Washington, and stayed with her for two weeks. I walked through my first true heartbreak on the dark blue rain-washed streets near the bay. I thought about all of the attractive girls that still worked at WildRidge, and was he working with them now? How about that one girl with the long dark hair and tattoos? I don't have any tattoos, and William had lots of them. He probably is with her. I hated the thought of it.

Asian Mom went to work during the day, and I sat at her apartment and looked at writing jobs in Tacoma. I applied to four of them. Asian Mom was recovering from, not only a divorce but an abusive relationship. Her husband counted her calories and told her that if she ate too much that day, she had to go for a run or do some sort of workout. She weighed less than ninety pounds when they divorced. They had two children together and one of them lived in Tacoma and worked at the local YMCA. She attempted to help me get a writing job at their corporate site. Out of the four places I applied, the YMCA was the only one polite enough to send a letter informing me that another candidate had been chosen. On my last night in Tacoma, I parked my vehicle on a side street downtown to get sushi with a friend who lived in Seattle at the time. When I returned, my truck's passenger side window was smashed in and my laptop stolen. Shattered glass covered the seat, door, and the floor. I drove back completely dejected. I had really failed this time. I messaged myself (to my laptop) and said, "Please just let me have my novel, you can keep the laptop."

Because I had started my first big project—a novel about a woman who had OCD. She was single, forty-one years old, and lived in Manhattan. Her name was Mia, and she was a lead scientist at a plant trying to solve the mystery of Alzheimer's disease for good. Mia had a group of scientists that she worked with, and each day, they committed countless hours to growing and testing plants that would heal Alzheimer's disease. What her group of scientists didn't know was that she was traveling to a nursing home to visit a man named Bill. She called him "Grandpa Bill," but he wasn't her grandpa. She convinced him that she was his granddaughter to deliver plant-derived medicines to heal him. The problem? Her medicines actually began to work, and soon, Grandpa Bill was able to verbalize that—no—this was not his granddaughter. The family discovers her and she gets sued. But was Mia actually doing any harm? She is taken to jail for trespassing and there she sits, in jail, with the answer to Alzheimer's disease. Will she be saved and the cure of Alzheimer's shared? Or will she, like so many individuals, remain stuck behind bars for a questionable injustice?

But all of that was gone now. All 45,600 words of it. Gone. It was probably being cleared off my laptop and brought to a pawn-shop. I called my brother—who always got so frustrated when his little sister was taken advantage of. He messaged my laptop and said, "Too bad, bro, you took the Sheriff's daughter's laptop. Good fuckin' luck."

I wasn't the Sheriff's daughter. But TJ and I had a good laugh about it, and then we talked, as we always did, about our life's struggles and successes. I thought sometimes that TJ had OCD. Growing up, he always needed things to be in order. His shoes. His jackets. His homework. I was a messy free spirit. But TJ needed everything clean and in-line. Maybe that's where some of my inspiration about Mia came from? Growing up with TJ.

In my family, there are the "girls" and "kids." We are chopped into two halves: same parents, two generations of children. There is almost a decade of time between my two oldest sisters "the girls" and my brother and I, "the kids." We attended a Presbyterian church when TJ and I were little, and when the helpers came to gather us for Sunday school, they told us that TJ had to go into one room (with the older kids), and I had to go into the other room (with the younger kids).

The helper lady said, "Emilee, you'll go here—with the three- to five-year-olds," and she waved an arm to a classroom with a short table with a half-circle cut out of it and little people chairs all around it. "TJ," she continued, "you'll go here, with the six- to eight-year-olds." His classroom had more kids in it, and they were loud.

He looked at his chaotic room and then back at me—and stared with big, terrified blue eyes. "Come on, TJ," the woman said, "you've gotta go over here."

TJ reached for my hand. When it made contact with mine, I could feel his were cold and clammy, and then he said, "I have to stay with her because she's my little sister."

The woman said that he couldn't stay with me because he was older. So, he lied. "She is older," he said, "she is actually six years old; she doesn't know how old she is."

I wondered if maybe this was true. I didn't know how old I was.

The lady said, "Okay, Emilee can go with you."

TJ acted like we had just escaped captivity together, and we had to get out of there fast before the enemy finds us again. He pushed me gently, the small backpack of crayons and coloring books on my back crunching, and said, "Come on, Em, we've gotta go to Sunday school in here today."

It was very obvious that I didn't belong in that classroom. The kids in my classroom were playing with blocks and eating snacks. In TJ's classroom, they actually had lessons. They were learning things, but I just wanted to play with blocks and eat snacks. They passed out these sheets where we had to write on them, and I didn't know how to write. I just sat there, silent, with my little pink backpack on and my feet dangling off the chair. I didn't know why TJ said I couldn't go into the other classroom, but here I was, with the older kids and totally out of place.

Being TJ's little sister put me in a lot of circumstances where I felt out of place, but at home next to him. TJ was born a popular kid. He was attractive, funny, smart, kind, and had all of the pre-reqs to be a popular kid. It's amazing how young the popular crowd forms. Elementary school is really when the draft happens. There arises a crew of people who only speak to others who look like them—perfect and desired. Naturally, they would all gravitate towards one another. I found myself floating along, but like a baby raft tied to a larger raft, into the crowd of popularity.

In high school, when I now had my own friends, TJ would call me and say that Mom wanted me to come home while I was staying a friend's house. "Mom wants me to come home?" I'd say.

"Yeah, she said you're supposed to come home now."

I didn't question it; I knew she never said that. It was him who wanted me to come home. So, I'd say, "Okay, well, I guess I need to come home then."

He'd respond, "I can come get you; I was going to run to the store anyway."

And I would say, "Okay."

His silver car would come screaming down the road twenty minutes later, and I'd get in, bass pounding deep and loud, and just so grateful that mother says I need to come home. I never asked my mother, me at fourteen years old and TJ at sixteen years old, if she requested that I come home.

TJ remained with the cool crowd, but always looking for me, with big wide eyes afraid of everything. He was terrified to be left, or to be alone. For his senior year photos, he requested that I be there for them. So, I got let out of high school to go sit in a dark studio with him while he got his senior photographs taken. When I had mine done two years later, he came with me, and we took photos together. He looked happier in my photos than his own—his were awful, because it wasn't a TJ smile. It was a fake smile.

As we grew older and time passed, I kept making decisions that terrified TJ. Falling seventy feet out of trees, moving to South Africa on a whim, traveling in Peru with ex drug dealers, and lots of other things that made him nervous. TJ kept things in order on organized shelves, clean walls, and his phone never had a single dent in it—he never used phone covers—because he didn't need them. He was methodical, funny, and when he would get stressed, I just wanted to hold his hands—cold and clammy as they were—and tell him it would all be okay.

BACK TO THE VALLEY I GO

Returning from Tacoma was a very hard thing to accept. I was headed back to the site of my heartbreak with a stolen laptop, or, I suppose, just without a laptop. In my therapy sessions, I began to learn how to focus less on William moving on and more on myself moving on with life. But what did that look like? I was still so intertwined with him. A few months later, I discovered that he had actually moved on—he started dating a mutual friend of ours who is a lot like me. She is a runner, funny, sweet, kind, and God it bothered me that he just found another ME. Why couldn't he date the girl with the long brown hair that has all the tattoos?? She was sexy, spirited, and seductive. At least it would confirm in me that we wouldn't have ever worked out. But no, here he is, dating someone just like me.

Over the months, I tried not to creep on her Instagram and Facebook—but she was creeping on mine. She watched every story I posted about me hiking mountains, running races, and starting my new job at a drug and alcohol abuse prevention center for youth. Maybe she thought my life was still sailing well on these stormy seas? It seemed liked it. And that's just the thing with social media—it always seems like people are doing better than they are. She was typically one of the first people to watch my stories, it felt like she was my number one fan. I continued in therapy until I couldn't afford the $150/session any longer. My job as program coordinator of a nonprofit became my new focus. However, my heart pulled me in a different direction. All I wanted to do was write. But how does one make a living just by writing?

My title as program coordinator meant that I went into affluent schools with kids doing drugs, that I could never afford myself, and try to convince them that other things were better. The girl before me seemed to love the position. I mean, genuinely. It's like when people talk about the relationship they're in; it's either a genuine "I'm in love and so happy," or it's disingenuous, and they still say that same phrase but with a counterfeit smile and everyone in the room can feel it. I was the counterfeit-smile happy person. I worked thirty hours a week, put together after-school events, and encouraged youth to get involved with sports. We went hiking, played soccer, practiced art, carved pumpkins, practiced music, and had a float in the Fourth of July parade down Main Street.

It would be an awesome position for somebody that's an extrovert. While running my after-school programs, I was simultaneously pitching articles to magazines, believing that I would never be good enough to write a novel. *Did I even want to write a novel?* I was more interested in nonfiction genres. Months after I accepted the position, I received some interesting news: the director, Amy, was quitting. She had had it with the board of directors. I got along very well with all of them and her. I thought Amy was a fantastic director, and the board were great supporters. But she said she needed out. When Amy left, she suggested to the board of directors that I take over. ME! A twenty-four-year-old confused girl with a broken heart and the greatest desire to just go live in the woods and write. I didn't even like teenagers. I sidestepped the responsibility, however, and agreed to take over during the interim. Since I was taking on more opportunity, I knew I should ask for more pay— but isn't that just the worst conversation to have ever? Even though I was sweating bullets, I dressed my best and walked into one the board member's law offices to request a raise from $19 an hour to $32 an hour. I didn't think they'd accept that much of a jump, but I was wrong. They unanimously agreed to pay me my requested amount.

I walked out of that office feeling like I was the smartest businesswoman in the world. With my huge pay raise and newfound commitment to the organization, I moved offices and waited for my new director to arrive. In the meantime, how do I process checks? I had to learn how to work with accounting, the board, and each of the schools. The new director requested more money than I could ever think of attaining *in my entire life*, and they accepted him.

AND, YES, THERE WAS ANOTHER GUY

He was more so in the background, but also the one that I actually wanted the entire time. The problem was that he didn't give me enough attention to even be mentioned in this book until now. We went climbing, hiking, and camping together, but never, not once, was there any interest from his side. From mine? It was flashing red like a stoplight... one of those stoplights that isn't working after a storm. So, you have to stop at it like a stop sign. Wait your turn.

His name was Clay. Clay was everything a girl like me could want—tall, handsome, gorgeous beard, videographer, Christian... but wait, did I still want a Christian? Was I even Christian? I wasn't sure. I was sure, however, that Clay was "The One" for me. We met at a rock-climbing festival and hit it off like fireworks. He drove a beefed-up truck and pulled over to set up the camera to capture scenes, which he was putting together for the founders of the festival.

I couldn't believe this was happening. A man that I thought I'd never have the opportunity to be with was actually spending time with me! We went everywhere together. We climbed a multi-pitch route that took us several hours to complete. Multi-pitches are climbed in sections because the length of the climb is longer than the length of the rope. The person on "lead," or the person that's clipping the clips to the bolts on the way up the route (or placing their own gear if they're climbing a traditional route without bolts), really needs to know what they're doing. They set the pace and the route for the crew. It was just Clay and I climbing this one, so we swapped sections. I led, and then he led, until there was a really hard section, where he asked, like a humble gentleman, if I wanted to take the lead on the hardest section.

"I have no ego about this," he said. "I think you're a little bit better climber than me."

I felt: A. like the hottest most badass chick in the world, B. like the hottest most badass chick in the world, and C. like the hottest most badass chick in the world.

I led the hard section, and then he followed me up. When we reached the same anchor point, he looked at me and said, "That was not an easy section. I'm impressed."

We reached the top and could see for miles and miles. He took more footage using his GoPro camera, and we did fifty push-ups on top of the mountain just to seal off the experience.

Clay and I seemed perfect for each other, but I wanted to play my cards right. I coached myself, saying, "Em, don't play too easy on this one. He gets a lot of attention from girls. Go hard on this one."

So, I didn't make it easy. He asked me to come hang out with him and his friends after our first weekend of climbing together, and I said I had to go back to Sun Valley for work. On the drive back to Sun Valley, I grew very disappointed in my decision. Was it right to say no? Did it leave him wanting more? Or less? Did I just show him I'm not interested when really I am? Should I tell him I'm interested? No, no, that's giving it all away. Play hard, Em. Play hard.

That was the only time I said no to spending time with Clay. The other times, I sacrificed plans with friends, drove twelve hours home from a climbing trip because he wanted to "get beers," and told people that we were getting married (he just didn't know it yet). Clay was an ultra-runner, which, how hot is that, also? I was a runner too, but I hadn't run more than a marathon. I was inspired by Clay and thought we could be this hot runner/climber/Christian couple and travel the world with him, shooting films and me writing books. It really was perfect—but there was a problem. Clay and I ran a race together, and when he completed the race, instead of running to me to celebrate—he chose to run next to me and collapse on the ground.

Let me paint this picture correctly for you: I'm done with my race because I ran the shorter version, and I've been done for about half an hour. It was a brutal race, up in the mountains and about ninety degrees of dry summer heat. People standing at the finish line talked about Clay and asked if we were together. I wasn't sure what to say, so I just said that we were running the race together. We waited and waited and waited, so the build-up of his arrival was growing greater and greater. Friends of his showed up at the finish line with beers. And there I was, standing in the middle of the dirt behind the finish line, waiting for him.

Finally, he came slowly, stepping down the last hill, and we all cheered. I'm ready to catch him with my arms wide open like those orange landing lights at the airport. Ya can't miss it. And what does he do? Completely ignore my existence and collapses on the ground next to me. The friends with the beer rushed over to help him stand up. I went from feeling like the most special, coolest chick on the mountain to the dumbest, most naïve one. We drove away in his truck and were silent. He asked if I needed to get anything from his house before I left for home, which was a three-hour drive.

Two months later, he asked me to come on another road trip with him. Same giddiness at the start, and it ended in the same sour disappointment. So, I decided that Clay might need a little nudge from me to display my interest in him. I signed up for the hardest race of my life. It was a 50k, which is thirty-one miles. The worst part about this race was it took place in the middle of February. Frozen, harsh ground, and more than a marathon. We ping-ponged comments back and forth about whether I would sign up for the race or not. Finally, I did it. I signed up to run thirty-one miles in the dead of an Idaho winter to prove to this man that I could run with the best of them. I was worthy of his love and affection. I really felt like this one would do the trick. It would be the magic to push us over the edge—into a real relationship. I mean, how many women can run thirty-two miles in negative temps?

My training regime for this race was very serious. Shorter mileage throughout the week (three to eight miles) and then longer runs on the weekends (twelve to twenty-five miles). Long-distance running is the perfect thing to do when you need to ponder life, for hours and hours. Clay was all I thought about as I trained for this 50k. I convinced myself that he did like me. He was just nervous and shy. Clay was a solo-roller like myself. I thought he would, eventually, warm up to the idea of me. Simultaneously, I signed up to do another thing that (I hoped) Clay would find attractive. I was going to be a yoga instructor. I signed up for a 200-hour yoga teacher training in Sun Valley, Idaho. *There*, I thought, *that will really do it*. A 50k-running (Christian) yoga instructor. She sounds unstoppable and like the perfect match for Mr. Clay.

Yoga teacher trainings are not cheap. This was thousands of dollars and hundreds of hours that I was committing to in exchange for the hope that Clay would find me just five percent more attractive. Of course, that's all fine and dandy when you're still making a lot of money for a twenty-four-year-old. I was still stackin' cash. Until I wasn't stackin' cash anymore and lost my job at the nonprofit. The board did everything they could to keep me, but funding was cut off, and the writing was on the wall—we were done. Immediately, I knew I had to cut the fat off of my life. The yoga teacher training had to go. I told the owner of the yoga studio, Kelly, that I had to be done.

"I'm so sorry," I said. "I just can't afford to continue with the program."

Her response, however, surprised me.

"No," she said. "You made a commitment, and remaining committed to this training will only help you make better choices in the future."

I was shocked. Kelly was a very kindhearted and sweet soul. I thought she'd allow me to drop, no problem, but she held firm. Embarrassed, I attended the first class and sat next to a woman named Ali. She was twenty-nine years old and looked like she was living her dream life. She was from Wisconsin and had recently moved to Sun Valley with her husband. He pulled up in this jet-black gorgeous truck to drop her off. He hunted, he was smart, he was kind, she was beautiful—and they seemed perfect to me.

Ali and I originally met in a one-stall bathroom. I always went pee right before going into a yoga class because I was not going to be one of those people who left during class. Apparently, she did the same thing. I left the door unlocked, and she came walking right in.

"Oh!" I said awkwardly.

Ali didn't look awkward at all—she just smiled and said, "Hi! I'm Ali!"

And then she shut the door and waited for me to be done. As I walked out, she said, "See ya in there!"

During class, in downward dog, she whispered to me, "I'm from Wisconsin and just moved here; we should be friends."

Still in downward dog, I whispered back, "I'm from Minnesota, I agree."

Ali and I were now in the same yoga teacher training, and I was learning much, much more about her life. Ali showed up to the first class with her pouch of essential oils and began taking them out and dabbing her wrists. She looked around to offer oils to others, "Lemongrass, peppermint, or lavender, anyone?" She took out a meditation pillow and placed it under her seat, getting comfortable. Then she pulled out a reusable bag filled with nuts and began munching on what looked to be Brazil nuts.

I was mesmerized by her. She operated in such a free way. I felt like every move that I made was filled with such anxiety about if it was or wasn't the correct move. It seemed like things just fell into place for her— she was a teacher, she was married, she had moved across the country, and now she was becoming a yoga instructor. I, on the other hand, had just lost my job, was literally chasing a man, and very concerned about every single move that I had made, was going to make, or even thought about making. Ali wanted to do "check-ins" with the group, time for each person to go around in a circle and share how they were feeling. Ali's "check-in" didn't reflect the perfect magical life I thought she had. Week after week, Ali shared more.

One evening, she welled up in tears and shared, "I feel like I gave away my freedom," she said, dropping her hands at her sides, "my husband is my best friend, but I just don't feel like I'm in love anymore. I want more. I want to go travel and do other things. I just committed my life to being a high school teacher and getting married because that's what I thought I was supposed to do."

She cried harder and held up her left hand, "I don't know if I want *this* anymore," she said, pointing to her wedding ring.

Well, that information was the ultimate shocker to me. Ali, the perfect life with the husband, wasn't happy either. What does happiness look like if it's not what she has? I was lost and so confused. And still training for my 50k, which I thought would get me the man, the ring, and the happiness. There was, of course, another problem—I felt like my leg was going to literally break from my femur. During a ten-mile run, I went up and down a mountain with this same splitting pain in my groin area. It was January, and my CamelBak water supply had turned into solid ice. With two miles left, I limped to my truck and cried when I finally made it.

I went to the doctor a week later and discovered the worst news for my run towards happiness with my mountain man, Clay. I had a stress fracture in my hip. What's worse? If I kept running on it, the fissure of a fracture would completely break through the femur, and I wouldn't be able to walk, let alone run, at all. My orders from the doctor were six weeks non-weight bearing. Crutches. Again. I was devastated and couldn't believe I'd have to tell my future husband that I couldn't run the race with him. Although, any excuse to call Clay was a good thing. I had to call him and tell him the news.

His response was lacking in many areas, including empathy, general care, or even listening ability. He was working on some project in his office when I called and, me, all emotional, told him the whole detailed story. He said, "Oh, no. I'm sorry," followed up by a, "Hey, I've got a client calling—can I call you back?"

"Sure! No problem!" I said, way too enthusiastic.

He called back about two hours later. We continued where we left off, which was right at the beginning.

"So, what happened?" he asked.

I replayed the entire dramatic story, including the frozen water pack, the determination, the pure grit to even make it ten miles on a fractured femur, and that I had to go into the doctor and she, the doctor a female, also said I'm a badass, but I couldn't keep running. I had to quit the race.

"Hm," he said. "That's too bad. Well, rest up! I might be up in your area in a few weeks or so, and maybe we can go for a hike—err, sorry, I mean just meet up."

I lived by those words, "just meet up," for the next few weeks, meditating on them daily. Clay was coming to visit me. Was it just a coincidence, or did he really want to see me? I was committed to believing that he was really, secretly, in love with me. He visited just as he said he would do—but made no specific effort to see me. He was there for work, filming a wedding, and was "on location." Being with him was, at this point, my entire identity, and the very thing that I'd been focusing on for the past two weeks, so I had to make it work. I limped my way out to my truck, clanked my crutches to the passenger-side door, and drove to visit him at this wedding he was filming. He was less than excited to see me show up and informed me that I should move my truck to another location because the wedding party was about to arrive. I left the wedding feeling completely worthless. He either had a super thick shell around his heart and I just needed to somehow melt the layers, or he truly wasn't interested in me.

The problem was me, I was sure of it. How could I fix this gaping issue of me not being good enough? Was it my personality? Was it the fact that I wore my father's flannels instead of new Patagonia flannels? Was it my teeth? My hair? My body? My beliefs? What was wrong with me? I couldn't figure it out, so I turned to my 24/7 therapist named Google. At seven p.m. on a Sunday night, with my second glass of wine, I googled, "How did you feel when you were 25?" I wasn't quite twenty-five yet, I was still twenty-four, but I figured, might as well see what's in store for me in the near future.

I found a blog post titled "25 and Feeling Lost?" I read the entire thing with a gripping connection. Wow! This girl was saying exactly the things that I felt. She was in a bad relationship and ended it. She lost her job. She moved across the country and felt like a failure—but then! She met her Prince Charming at twenty-nine years old. I had to wait another four years? I could do that, I could wait four more years if my dream life would be delivered to me via express same-day shipping when I turned twenty-nine.

It was something to hold onto, so I changed all of my passwords to include something with the number "29" in the code. I literally began manifesting my twenty-ninth year on this earth to be the best year of my life. It might be a shit storm until I get there, but when I reach twenty-nine, it will be a glossy clear lake on a cloudy day. I would view my reflection in the still waters of my life and see my face, my beautiful face, standing between me and my cloudy judgment and challenges. I was taking back my life, and it would get better, just not for another four more years.

Four More Years of This Shit

That's kind of a long time—four years. What was I going to do with the next four years of my life until I found the peachy freedom of being twenty-nine? Well, I figured, since relationships don't matter, I'd just sort of "mess around," and as long as the men included in my messing around know there is no chance at actually being with me, then it's harmless, right?

But, wait, Ali is twenty-nine.

One afternoon, Ali called and said, "What are you doing?"

I had biked to a bridge between Hailey and Ketchum and was about to get into the Bigwood River. I got off my bike and set it against the bridge's wooden railing.

"I'm gonna get in this river," I said. "What are you doing?"

"I'm going to the courthouse and filing these divorce papers."

"Holy shit," I said. "Fuck. Okay, come here after?"

Ali began to tear up and, through a strained voice, said, "Okay."

I wasn't sure what to say. I hadn't been in this position before. I thought it was all working out for her, but apparently, it wasn't. When

126

Ali arrived at the bridge, we both submerged ourselves in the cool river water and watched the waves roll over our bodies.

"I don't know where to go from here," she said. "But somehow," she smiled at me, "somehow, I know I did the right thing. I just..." she threw her arms wide open into the air and said, "I just feel free again!"

Ali slid into the water like a baby seal and popped back out to climb on top of a log.

I climbed out of the water to sit atop the log next to Ali, and we made a decision for ourselves, and together—we would choose the path that feels right. Not the one we "think we're supposed to take," or the "one that everyone else is taking," but the path that we authentically wanted to take.

There was just one problem—what in the world did that path look like?

I didn't feel an overwhelming calling to be married or have children. But that's what I felt I was supposed to do because all the families that did that looked happy on social media. Their sparkling diamond rings, wedding songs, and family photos all looked to me like the epitome of happiness. If that's not where my happiness can be found, then where is it?

Ali and I went to many different sites of water, including rivers, hot springs, swimming pools... we just found water and got inside of it. We both wanted not only to be in water, but to be water. The element of movement and the ultimate force that can heal and smooth the roughest of surfaces. We submerged our jagged perspectives into rushing waters hoping that the effect on us would be to soothe our hurting and broken parts. Like a stone picked from the spine of the riverbed that's been carried, rolled, shaped, broken, molded, and now—found perfect for picking. Perfect for holding. Or, if the one who picks it decides, once again, to skip the perfectly smooth rock across the mirror of a lake's surface, it will sink to the bottom and grow even softer yet.

Over the next few months of yoga teacher training, I hobbled in on my crutches and clanked them side by side as I sat on blankets and bolsters. My body was conditioned to run and be free. To grip my toes into the rocky-mountainside and run with a forward motion away from all of the rejection, hurt, and aching insecurities that I Am Not Enough. The hope of being with Clay dangled in front of me like "the thing" I had to achieve in order for the rejection, hurt, and aching insecurities to disappear. They would, I thought, just dissolve—if I could spend forever with him. Yoga teacher training is the exact opposite of running from, it is a complete surrender and sit still sort of practice.

I looked ahead on our yoga schedule and discovered my greatest fear. Yin yoga coincided with my stress fracture. Yin yoga is one of the slowest styles of yoga. It involves more meditative practices, breath work, and sitting in relaxed postures for up to five minutes at a time. This would've been okay if I had run seven miles before the class and seven miles after the class. Instead, I had to just sit. And sit and sit and sit. Kelly brought in a special instructor from L.A. to speak to us about Yin, meditation, and slowing down. I told her I can't slow down; my body needs to be in forward motion. That's just who I am. Sitting here on the floor and doing nothing for hours on end wasn't going to work for me. She was bald with dark chocolate skin and looked like a goddess with light white strips of fabric flowing behind her in the wind as she stepped into the small studio. Her voice was even goddess-like, deep, and melodic. She told me that slowing down is exactly what I needed, if it was, in fact, the very thing I wanted to run from. What are you running from? She would ask.

Trying to be more relaxed like Ali, I took out my snacks and began to munch during one of her teaching sessions. She paused, looked at me with surprise, and said, "What is it that makes you feel like you need to eat right now?" I was confused, and responded with honesty, "It's seven-thirty and we've been here since five this evening."

"You should really think about why you're telling your body that you need to eat right now." The other twelve ladies in the course felt just as awkward as me, I could feel the energy in the room shift. So, I put my snacks away and then when I got home at nine-thirty that evening, I ate three bowls of cereal, a peanut butter and banana sandwich, a whole chocolate bar, and finished it off with a glass of wine. Why would she tell me I can't eat? I eat when I'm hungry. I ate until my stomach hurt and I could barely sleep. Sitting up, because I couldn't lay in bed, I thought about what she said. Was I just eating because it was "time to eat?" Was I really hungry? This is all witchcraft, I decided. Of course, I was hungry, it was dinner time! But my witch side perked up, maybe we tell ourselves we're hungry when we look at the clock. Oh, it's noon? Time for lunch. Oh, it's six? Time for dinner. Then I asked myself this: If I were living on a remote island without a watch, would I have been hungry? I decided, that, yes, I would have been.

However, the situation with the goddess food police did make me question my eating habits. I didn't want to admit it, but I was struggling with food. I would starve myself all day, feeling thin, light, and happy in my skin—and then when I got home, I'd binge eat. A whole bag of chips, a row of Oreos, half a box of cereal, an entire jar of peanut butter. You don't go into it thinking you're going to eat the entire thing; it starts with one bite. Like with the peanut butter, for example, I opened a fresh jar of Jif (the small one, not the family size) and began eating respectable spoonfuls of peanut butter. And then I'd just wondered, *what's on the television*? So, I'd turn the T.V. on and watch the current show of filthy drama that I was obsessed with at the time and then, before I knew it, almost the entire jar was gone. Like magic. It's gone. The worst one was probably the time I ate an entire half gallon of ice cream. It was over the course of two days, but the spoonful trick got me again. Just one more spoonful...

Goddess food police was right. I wasn't listening to my body; I was stress eating. What made me come under some spell and eat until I was sick? Figuring that I'm an emotionally and spiritually aware individual, I thought I could just light some candles and have a serious conversation with myself—but this had been a problem of mine for years. How was I going to stop it? I started adding an orange check mark on my calendar to each day that I went without binge eating. Monday—orange check, Tuesday—fail, Wednesday—fail, Thursday—orange check, Friday—fail. My weeks weren't looking too good, and I was gaining weight fast, especially now that I couldn't run it off. What was even more embarrassing was that I was in yoga teacher training. Being a yoga instructor was basically like you had to be a model. You had to be sexy, sleek, and way more fit than everyone else in the room. My weight gain definitely didn't make me feel like the sexy, sleek, way more fit individual. I was the left-behind, broken, and on crutches, fatty.

The Sun Valley seasons slipped from fall to winter and the 50k happened without me. Clay posted photos of finishing the February-frigid 50k, and I just knew I'd missed my chance at forever. My body had failed me. Hobbling back and forth from my yoga teacher training classes to my two-bedroom condo, I didn't know how to change myself, but I knew I needed change. I am better than this, I said to myself. How do I exude the confidence that other women seem to naturally have? How do I create a better life for myself? One that's not so self-deprecating?

I sat down with a piece of paper and wrote: Speak your truth. And then I said it out loud to myself like a rehearsal: Speak your truth. Speak your truth. Speak your truth. What do does Emilee want? Speak your truth.

Pen in hand, I wrote down one word: Travel.

Travel Is the Answer

I decided I'd feed my soul and give my emotional eating habits a break—I'd travel. I wanted my feet to be dirty, my mind to be working, and my heart to be happy again. With $2,008 in my bank account, I contacted a nonprofit that I'd done some editing work for in the past and said I wanted to volunteer my time to go to Tanzania.

"That's perfect," the executive director, Maria, said. "We need someone to travel to Tanzania and capture the students' stories. I think you'd be a great person for that job."

A month later, with my yoga teacher training completed, I flew out to Tanzania with my big red backpack and a shining heart. After waiting for two hours to get through customs in the Tanzanian airport, I located a man holding a sign reflecting the name of the nonprofit. The man, named Mosi, had the biggest smile on his face—welcoming me into this old converted fourteen-passenger van to take me to their guest house. Just like being in the fourteen-passenger van heading out to the desert at WildRidge, I was once again in a snapshot moment, in another van, heading towards a village with dirt kicking up behind the van and a happy driver.

"You ever been to Africa," Mosi asked, smiling still so brightly and looking at me in the rearview mirror.

"Yes," I said, "I've been to South Africa, but never to Tanzania."

"Oh," he said, delighted, "Welcome!"

The van rocked side to side over bumps and dips in the road, moving fast ahead toward an orange setting sun that faded into the sky and melted onto dry African red-dirt. My plans for this nonprofit were quite ambitious—I wanted to write grants, raise awareness, and capture all of the twelve students' stories in less than one month. When we arrived, a group of people welcomed me. The cook, the housekeeper, the student visiting from college, and the night guard. Wait, *night guard*? The entire guest house, which was only a few bedrooms, a kitchen, and a living room, were enclosed by tall strong walls with a gate where Mosi and I drove through. It was protected at night by an armed night guard. It wasn't, I noticed, in the safest of areas. But that's the whole point of being located here, right?

Mount Kilimanjaro rose above the guest house in the distance like King Kong overlooking the busy little nation of Tanzania. I dreamed of climbing Kili, but didn't have anywhere near enough money to do so. Each morning began with Swahili lessons from the college student currently staying at the house. Then, I'd walk two miles into town with the housekeeper to gather vegetables for the week's meals and walk with her the two miles back.

We eventually fell into a rhythm of life, with me visiting the kids at their boarding school and meeting with them one on one to capture their life stories. Most of the kids were between the ages of twelve to eighteen and had lost one or both parents to disease, genocide, addiction to drugs or alcohol, or other traumatic events. They were chosen to join this group of kids to receive sponsorship to attend a better school, and therefore give them a chance at a better life. The public schools were overflowing. Brick walls were broken, and the play-yard was overgrown with grass, revealing patches of dirt where students congregated most often. There were so many children running every which way—but the boarding school in Tanzania wasn't like that. Those kids took their dirty, worn shoes off at the entryway of each classroom and lined them up perfectly. They had organized schedules, a computer lab, and some donated books. Though they weren't new, fancy computers—they had them. And though they weren't new, clean books—they had them.

These children went from being counted among the least to succeed in their villages to among the most likely. They were quiet, humble, and even when their school day was over, were putting in extra time working on their studies. These students didn't take their opportunity at higher education lightly, and therefore wanted to be doctors that healed, lawyers that changed unfair policies, nurses that cared for the sick, engineers to improve Tanzania's infrastructure, and teachers to give others the opportunity they'd now been given.

As I was meeting with these kids over a series of three weeks, I once again became very strikingly aware of my white privilege. Growing up as a middle-class, white female in America, I felt I could do anything I wanted. Yes, we as women have had our own battles with fairness and equality, but I never looked subjectively at my country and felt a call to pursue a profession that would improve the nation's lacking healthcare system, infrastructure, or educational system. There are, of course, things that can be done to improve America's system, but I didn't feel the pressures of America's future resting on my shoulders. These kids felt those pressures, and they were accepting the call. I couldn't imagine what that would feel like, to walk several miles back to your village wearing boarding school khakis and a tie, past all of your public-school peers running rampant without direction, proper nutrition, or support.

Some of my friends from home would ask, "Why must you travel so far to help others when there are plenty of children that need help in America?" It was, in no way, on the same playing field. The poverty in America was not the poverty in Africa. The extreme poverty of Africa does not diminish the extreme poverty in America, but they were not on the same scale. I wasn't sure how to explain that, nor could I find the truth within myself to discover what my attraction to African nations was? Why did I love it here so much? Why did I feel at home? I did what I always do when I'm trying to process something... I wrote about it.

What Is It About Africa?

I sat down with the twelve kids' stories that I'd written and a blank sheet of paper for me to process. What was it about these kids' lives? Why did I feel more connected to the red African dirt than the blood-shed American soil? My father raised us to understand that our freedom was not free. I felt great pride for America and honored to be my father's daughter. Though for some odd ancestral reason, I didn't feel like a descendent of Americans. I felt like a descendent of Africans. However, I didn't know why, and I thought it sounded really weird to say that out loud—so I dove deeper into it. What was it about the African culture that drew me in so intensely?

Here's what I came up with: compassion, spirituality, and culture. Africans carried a deep, burning compassion for their brothers and sisters—everyone was welcome at their table. Even if they didn't have enough food, they would pray. Which leads right into spirituality. I heard a quote once that said, "Americans *like* God, Africans *need* God." Americans like going to church, Americans like spending time in Bible studies, and Americans like growing deeper in their faith. Africans, however, need God to survive. They would pray, earnestly, for God to provide enough food for them, their families, and their guests. And even if they were struggling to survive, they held high their pride of Africa. I remember some of the shacks I visited in South Africa had beautiful African prints hung up on the walls, covering windows that had been broken in or doors that didn't shut. They were proud to be from the Nation of Africa whose colors were so bright, whose people were so welcoming, and whose culture banded together. It felt as though I'd found true community in African nations, whereas America was sectioned. People in America lived their own little lives separate from one another, in their homes and barely speaking to neighbors. People in America seemed to compete and compare; people in Africa seemed to collaborate and care for one another. Of course, this is a massive generalization because North America and Africa are very large and diverse places, but it had been my experience—with the small spaces of both places that I'd had the opportunity to visit and make a life within.

But was it okay for me to even feel this way? I hadn't experienced the same struggle, and I was fearful of appearing as the "White Savior" during my overseas volunteering expeditions. Besides Americans telling me that there were more than enough Americans that needed help, and I need not travel to another country—I was also told that not all of Africa is living in poverty, and some countries are richer than parts of America. This was true, in some respects. Among the richest in Africa are Nigeria and South Africa. So, my speculative onlookers would question, why are you seeking to help one of the richest countries on the African continent (while I was traveling in South Africa)? Great question, I'd say. I guess they'll never understand the intense levels of poverty that can exist just blocks away from mansion homes with spikes on top of their fences meant to keep the impoverished people out.

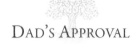

DAD'S APPROVAL

When I finally returned to America from Tanzania, I went right back into my peacock-persuasive dance with Clay. His family, being hyper-Christian, loved my missionary stories. During my travels in Tanzania, I had met several young people starting businesses sewing shoes, growing coffee, and making hand-woven bags. It was my goal to start a store back in Idaho and sell their goods, thereby increasing profits to grow their businesses. Clay's father thought it was a brilliant idea, and upon first mention—told me he would invest financially in my overseas business. I was starting the next World Market, or so I thought.

"Wouldn't this be great?" I said to Clay with stars in my eyes.

He was silent. Which, was right in-line with his typical character of clearly appearing to not have any interest in me. But I was here? In his house? With his family? Of which! HE invited me! *There had to be some interest*, I said to myself. Soon after his father told his mother who told his sister who told his other sister who told their brother, and was I really starting to believe that I'd be a part of their family one day.

Clay gave no interest, so instead of carrying on the one-sided conversation, I decided to drive back home. On the drive, Clay called and said it's not a good idea.

"I've watched my dad get involved in businesses with friends before and it can get messy, so I'd rather that not happen," he said. "It's best to not mix friends and family with business."

Mix *friends* and family?

Alright, I decided, he must be gay. Poor thing, just cannot come out of the closet to his hyper-Christian family. I waited and waited and waited until finally, one year later, he came to visit me on my birthday.

TWENTY-FIVE BIRTHDAY SURPRISE

I thought this was the day, my twenty-fifth birthday. He was going to ask me to be his girlfriend. *At least!* It coincided with my cousin's husband, Jason's birthday, who was turning thirty. He planned a big birthday gathering for his "dirty thirty" birthday, and we all went to these stunning hot springs in the mountains. It was the perfect setup—for complete and utter disappointment.

With snow lightly falling down around us, Clay drove me back to my house in Sun Valley. I wanted so badly to hold his hand and just set my seat back and relax. But he looked very serious.

"I want to talk to you about something," he said. "Some people have been talking, and I know you kind of want this to be more than a friendship."

My heart starting pitter-pattering, but not the good kind. I knew by his tone what was coming next.

"I just feel like I need to be honest with you," he said. "I thought about it, prayed about it, and I just don't think it's there for us," he said.

I looked out the window at the sparkling snow, but now it had a different effect. It wasn't dreamy anymore. It was sad. It was shattered bits of my perfectly blue sky raining down around us.

We made it back to my house, and he suggested we watch the Super Bowl together. This confused my brain greatly, but I knew what I needed at that moment and asked for it.

"I need to be alone for a while," I said. "Thanks for coming to the birthday party," I said.

"So, I should just go home?" he asked.

"Yes," I said. "Please just go home."

I went to Avia and Jason's house and sat in the living room, completely broken and in tears. Clay, it turned out, didn't want to and never wanted to be with me. This has a very intense impact on someone who doesn't quite understand how to separate the events of their life from the value they hold. My value was held in being with Clay. If I could secure a strong mountain man, I thought, that would give me belonging and purpose. People will want to be friends with me and ask me how I found such an amazing man. How *we* have such a perfect relationship. What were our secrets?

When I first moved out to Idaho as a bright-eyed twenty-two-year-old, I thought that life would just fall into place. I thought I'd keep getting better at rock climbing, and my community would grow. Naturally, the mountain man with the beard and the truck would appear—which he did—and we would get married. It would be a beautiful mountain wedding, and all of my friends from Minnesota would be so inspired to make changes in their lives that made them happier. I would have succeeded in moving across the country by myself and making a life. But what was this? This was a mess of a life. The same message that rang from the hang-up with William rang me again—I. Am. Not. Good. Enough. Not Christian and calm enough to make the relationship with Mike work. Too high of standards to make the relationship with William work. And simply, downright, not attractive or clean or strong or athletic or successful enough to be with Clay. I was a misfit. And what does a misfit do, but pack up all of their belongings into a truck and drive far, far away?

The driving far, far away part, however, didn't happen right away. I spent another year in Sun Valley trying to meet new friends, dating all types of men, and really opening myself up to new world of pleasure. I began to ask myself: *why am I saving my virginity for some man on a white horse to come along and take it from me*? It's mine and I get to do whatever I want with it, especially to let it go and break the rules for once.

And then I met Trent.

I positioned myself, thoughtfully, as a damsel in distress—alone at the rock-climbing gym and desperate. Trent was climbing with another guy named Dustin. I wasn't interested in Dustin, though, I was interested in Trent. The one with the mountain tattoo on his arm that peeked out from underneath his shirt as he climbed. Trent looked rough, with tough skin and disheveled blonde hair peeking out from under a beanie. Candy green eyes that were far from innocent.

"Hey," I said, walking over to them, "could I bum a climb from y'all?" Trent suddenly looked nervous—a bad boy who gets nervous—I shall proceed.

As if timing had worked out perfectly in our favor, Dustin tells us he was headed out to meet his girlfriend for dinner. "I'll belay you," Trent said. And then tossed a little wave to Dustin as he walked off to remove his rock-climbing gear.

Trent made me feel something new. Danger. Danger. Danger. And I liked it, because he was not only Danger, but also a kind-hearted man. He had a soft smile, and I was curious about his past, because I felt that it was heavy.

"Where are you from?" He asked.

"I'm from Minnesota," I said. "You?"

"I'm from here—*the Valley*."

It was the way he said "*the Valley*" that kind of just made me turn warm and tingly inside. I was certain where this was headed now because we were both all of a sudden like shy middle school children. All nervous and jerky. Talking fast and then apologizing even faster. Brushing one another's arm and then apologizing for something as simple as speaking. We climbed a few climbs and then exchanged phone numbers. The next day, he invited me to visit some hot springs with him. There was just one request he had—could I drive?

Odd date, I thought. A guy has never asked me to pick him up. They're really progressive out here in the West. When I picked him up, at his mother's house, he said there was something that I needed to know about him.

"I can't drive," he said. "Because I have a DUI."

"Oh shit," I said. "I'm sorry to hear that. For how long?"

"Five years."

"You can't drive for five years??"

"Well, I have five DUIs."

At the start of this conversation, I thought it was kind of a funny little story that he had a DUI, a lot of people get a DUI. Not a lot of people have five DUIs.

"Yeah, so I just got out of jail and am under surveillance and stuff."

I tried to imagine what life would be like with a boyfriend who can't drive. I would have to drive everywhere. And forget my drinking and carousing at night, he can't drink. Not even a drop of Kombucha, out of fear that he'd get randomly drug tested. I didn't know how I felt about our future together anymore, but we were here—headed down this dirt road to a hot spring.

The more I learned about Trent, the more I liked him. He was real and raw. He biked to my house every day; it was kind of nostalgic. I never had a boy bike to my house in middle or high school just to see me. But now, at twenty-five years old, a hot rock climber with five DUIs and a tattoo of the Idaho mountains on his arm was biking to my house just to see me. I could tell that he was a little embarrassed about it, when I'd open the door and his face was frozen with pink cheeks and full swollen lips. His green jacket zipped all the way up, leaving just enough space for him to breathe. Trent always brought his bike into my little condo that I'd somehow scored with another friend of mine, and placed it upside down like they do at the bike shops. Trent was a carpenter, I soon discovered. And that made him even more attractive.

Trent was twenty-eight years old when we met, and didn't have much patience for my interest in remaining pure. Which, I never verbalized, he could just tell. I would let things get a little out of hand (*exciting!*), but never too out of hand, and would always stop us before things got too far.

His lips were really delicious though, and I wanted to keep kissing them. We kissed for hours, it felt, until he finally asked, "Why won't you have sex with me?"

Silence.

And then I responded the way that a strong, independent female would respond: "I don't know."

And so that's how that happened.

Sex with Trent would improve over time, but it wasn't great the first time. It was awkward for both of us. It happened on a random mid-week afternoon, with sunlight streaking in through my blinds, and we were both sober as purified water. It was choppy, and anti-climactic.

But I had accomplished the task of releasing my virginity to the wild. It was lost now, and I would forever be a new person, an untamed woman, or something like that. Soon, Trent and I were a thing, and I had to tell all the other boys I had been playing around with that the games were over. I had a boyfriend now. Trent and I didn't like to be away from each other, so he stayed at my place, and I stayed at his mother's place. We slept in adjacent bedrooms, his mother and Trent and I. His mother was a lot like me—a gypsy yoga person. Walking around the house, which I soon had the code to and would let out their dog in the middle of the day, made me feel understood. There were yoga symbols on watercolor artwork, round Buddha statues placed about, and lots of plants. I was now working at a small coffee shop as a barista, and Trent would bike over on his lunch break to have a muffin and coffee with me. He made my heart beat faster each time I saw him, or slept with him, or thought about him.

They say it takes a few months to truly get to know a person. This was true for Trent and me because after four months I thought I knew him well. He was a nice man with a disease that is called addiction to alcohol and he was breaking that cycle forever. I found him very inspiring, and his past didn't worry me one bit. It made me love him more, until he got his own place.

Maybe he just couldn't bear to release his silent anger in front of his sweet and kind mother. His mother had been divorced from his alcoholic father since he was in middle school. Trent still loved his father but resented him for breaking up their family. He didn't know how to cope with the pain and therefore followed right down the path his father set before him. The first time his anger surfaced was in the middle of the night. After sex, he got up, peed with the door open, and came back and laid down next to me. He began scrolling through social media on his phone. I thought this was very cold, after I just shared my body with him. In the blue-white light of his screen, he turned and looked at me with a pitiful smile.

"You should go home," he said.

"What?" I said, "It's three in the morning."

He began to laugh at me as if I truly were a joke. "Yeah, well, this is my apartment and I want you to leave."

"Why?" I asked.

"Because I just don't want you here anymore! Go!"

I felt like a prostitute walking out of that dank apartment building, down the stained carpeted stairwell, and out onto the cold night street. I climbed into my truck, and drove home in silence. Before I could make it ten minutes away, Trent text me saying, "I'm sorry, come back."

What the fuck?" I said out loud, and then chose not to respond.

The next day, my doorbell rang.

It was Trent, with a dozen red roses.

"I'm so sorry," he said. "I don't know what was wrong with me last night, I was really a douche to you."

"Yeah," I said, "you were."

"Will you forgive me?"

He looked like a sad man with a big heart, and one who just couldn't click the pieces of his broken past into place. I knew what forgiveness meant, and I chose to oblige.

He gave me the roses, said he would call me later, and left.

Now, this is always an interesting spot to be at in a new relationship—to ask oneself—is this a mistake or a pattern? Is this something that will change or not? Should I believe him or run now? I chose to stay, for a little while longer, but created some nice distance between us.

I invited Ali to go to the hot springs with me, I needed a sister's advice.

"What a fuckin' prick," she said, holding a box of organic wine and drinking straight from the spout. "I'd drop that one, you're hot, don't settle for that shit."

When we drove back in town, we stopped at a burger joint. "My friends are going to meet us here," Ali said, "I'm going home with one of them."

"Which one?" I said.

"Jax. You'll know who he is as soon as you see him. We've been hooking up here and there."

"Do you like him?" I asked, like a five-year-old.

"I don't know what I feel anymore," she said. "He could invite his photographer friend? Do you want to meet him?"

I thought about Trent, and then I felt a red-hot anger rise from within me, maybe jealousy or betrayal, and I said, "Yes, invite the photographer friend."

His name was Jarron.

Jarron talked a lot about photography. It was engaging for about twelve minutes. Ali and Jax were all cozy and flirtatious, and then they were gone. It was just Jarron and me.

"Do you want to come over to my place? There's a jacuzzi."

I figured, why not? What's the harm? I shouldn't be driving right now anyway. So, we left my truck at the burger joint, and we went to his place. A little nicer than Trent's, but not a lot nicer. We tiptoed across the cold parking lot, and opened the fence to get into the apartment's outdoor jacuzzi.

We forced conversation, with him moving closer and closer, giggling at things that weren't in the least bit funny such as "I enjoy rock climbing."

Bubbles cleared out of the way until he was right next to me. I looked around to see if suddenly the jacuzzi had shrunk and there was no more space for the guy, besides right next to me.

"Wanna go back?" he whispered, the hoppy smell of beer on his breath.

"Sure!" I said, and hopped out way faster than he expected.

We sprinted back across the parking lot, and took our turns in the shower. I went first. Showers are a fantastic time to check in with oneself, and I found myself asking me if I would have sex with this man. He was very *Portland*, with tan skin and a moustache. Clean cut and also looking like a sex offender at the same time.

When I got out, he didn't seem to be flirtatious anymore, and began talking about all the STDs going around the Valley because everyone is hooking up with everyone else. I thought that was gross, and a definite turn-off. He showered, and I perused, walking from the modest kitchen with wooden bowls and stacks of mail on a small island to the living room. The television sat in the corner unplugged. He had a shelf of books including philosophy and classic reads like *Walden*, *The Odyssey*, and *For Whom the Bell Tolls*. There were a lot of cool looking rocks, ones that a geologist would have in their home or study. When he came out of the shower, he noticed I was looking at his rock collection.

"Pretty cool stuff, huh?" he said.

"Yeah," I said. "Pretty rocks!"

He sat down on the futon and carried on with a twenty-minute story about where he found them, what they were, and why they were special. He then pulled out a picture-book of rocks in Idaho and flipped through it telling me where I'd find them, as if I had asked him where I could find them.

"I'm pretty tired," I said. "I'll sleep out here on the futon, thanks for having me over."

"Yeah, of course," he said. "Let me get you some blankets."

I sat down on the futon with a sign of relief, we weren't going to have sex. We were going to sleep in separate rooms, and I felt good about that. Until he came back, leaned over me on the couch and began making out with my face like we were in a race with other couples. Devouring my face. Things were still a little fuzzy from the alcohol and a lot of hot water that drained my energy and hydration, but I knew what would happen and I had no interest in putting in the energy to stop it. I wasn't interested in Jarron. Technically, I was still dating Trent.

He pulled me from the futon to his bed, the next room over. And what happened next lasted longer than I wanted it to. He was like an artist in bed, wanting to make sure all details were covered. I just wanted it to be over. We fell asleep, and then he woke me up at six fifteen in the morning, with kisses and coffee.

"Good morning, love," he said, with his chest hair popping out of a robe.

"What time is it?" I said, rolling over.

"A little after six," he said. "You can go back to sleep if you want, I just wanted to make love one more time before going to work. Last night was amazing."

I propped up on one elbow, with the bed sheets falling down around my bare chest. "Maybe later," I said, doing my best to display a sleepy-sexy smile. "I need some rest."

"No worries, hot stuff," he said. "Sleep as long as you'd like, I'll be home around four this afternoon."

I found a ride to my truck as soon as he was out of the parking lot. I couldn't remember if we had exchanged numbers, but apparently, we hadn't, because he sent me a message on Instagram.

It read, "That was the best night I've had in a long time, when can I see you next?"

As I was reading his message, Trent called.

"Hey babe," Trent said, "want to meet at the coffee shop?"

"Sure," I said.

And then I immediately wondered what I was going to say to him. Should I tell him? Should I not? Maybe this was my way out?

We arrived at the exact same time. Me parking my truck and him locking his bike to a bike rack. We walked in and ordered together. He paid. We sat down and neither of us had a lot to say, so we just sipped our hot coffees too fast so that it burned our lips. I didn't do well finessing this transition, so I just blurted it out.

"I kind of hooked up with someone last night," I said.

He stared at me. "Like, you had sex?"

I nodded once.

"With who?" he asked.

"That doesn't matter," I said. "It happened."

"Well, I'm sure I know the dude, this is a small town, you know."

"I know."

"Why did it happen?"

Silence.

"I don't know," I said.

After a few more moments of silence, he stood up and walked out of the coffee shop, got on his bike, and rode away. I sat there, relieved.

Trent and I met only a few times after that, to say we were sorry. I apologized for hooking up with another dude, and he apologized for how he treated me. Jarron soon understood that I couldn't keep seeing him, either. There wasn't a spot in my life for these men—just a few spaces in time like stamps revealing that I didn't know what I was worth. I felt disenchanted about the whole thing. Love was reduced to sex, and sex was transactional. I give sex, I get "love." I share my body, I get belonging. The problem with that understanding of love is that is just isn't true love. It's moment-to-moment physical relief, like using another person for your own selfish desires. I had escaped these loose ends with less trust in myself, no trust in men, but thankfully, a clean STD record. Dodging bullets, left and right, just hoping my great luck would continue.

AM I EVEN MEANT FOR MONOGAMY?

Perhaps, I was meant to have little sparks of short-term relationships? None of these attempts at long-term relationships were working, so I decided to accept the true gypsy side of myself. I would forever be a free spirit and date whomever I wanted. Sometimes they might overlap with other men, and they would be okay with it, because that's how they were too. We were all free.

The next year was filled with lots of sexual experiences and even more confusion. It did not make me feel free—it made me feel empty and lonely—shackled to the void.

I couldn't take it anymore. I needed to escape my drunken hook-up memories, the hurtful rejection of Clay, and the way I'd now found myself teetering in and out of a relationship with a man thirteen years older than myself. He wasn't so down with my free-spirited nature, and wanted me and only me, and all of me to himself. He was a smart businessman who helped me grow my writing business. I never planned to date this man, named Wilson, or "Willy" as they all called him, but here we were—sleeping together and I was meeting his two children. I never wanted to meet his kids, but it happened, and now they referred to me as their father's girlfriend. Does one correct a four-year-old? *Nope, sweetie, I am not your father's girlfriend, just a silly mess-up one drunken night that I greatly regret.*

Clearly, I didn't have the heart to do that, and my starving bank account was greatly benefitting from this man's support. He helped me believe in myself, and charge what I was worth. At twenty-five years old, I was running my own business—a writing business—and it was growing. Willy told me to charge three times what I was charging, and my clients accepted. They told me they were happy to pay more, because I should have been charging more all along. That feedback made me feel secure in myself and my work. I began to notice the disparity between what men charged and what women charged for their services, men always being greater. It was like men had been given a different sheet to look at for what they were worth. Why didn't I just step right into my career and charge what I am worth? It took a man coming along to tell me what I am worth, as if he revealed his secret sheet of numbers to me and shared that I need not make myself so small.

Soon, we were traveling around doing speaking engagements and planning an empire. I was meeting with VPs and CEOs and people whose titles I had to search on Google before we met. People were contacting me and wanted to work with me on their big idea projects, saying I am just the right person. Though I didn't even know that I was the right person, and I felt indebted to Willy for all of this. My disgust for being in a relationship with him kept growing, and my strength to stand on my own and apart from his man-sheet of numbers revealing what I was worth as a human, kept diminishing. It was like all of this gold had been revealed, but he had the key to show me to the gold. And he would take me there, to this hidden place filled with golden treasures, I just have to accept him as a sexual partner in life first.

Meanwhile, his ex-wife and his ex-wife's mother were stalking me and telling me that he is an awful human and I should leave now while I still can. The two were in an intense custody battle during our confusing situation, and Willy asked me to be there for him during his court proceeding. He wrote things on note cards, ate organic food, drank nothing but pH-balanced water, and paced the house practicing for his court date.

As soon as it was over, he drove to my condo, a two-hour drive from Boise, got into my dry bathtub, and cried.

"They're taking my babies from me," he said through tears. "This is so fucking unfair; the court system favors women just because they are the mothers. She has no job, she is hanging out with some trashy dude, and they're going to send my two beautiful babies to be with her and I have to pay child support??"

He was stunned. I was stunned. And I had no idea what to say or think besides the fact I shouldn't be the one trying to help this recently divorced man.

"I'm so sorry," I said.

He looked at me and said, "You are beyond the greatest thing that has happened to me, I love you, and I will never leave you."

My stomach dropped. I didn't love this man. I didn't even want to be in a relationship with this man. I felt I had to tell him.

"I am so glad I could be here for you," I said. "But I am not interested in being in a relationship with you, and I was clear about that from the beginning."

"Well," he said, "Things are different now. We are business partners, and you can't just leave me here."

"How are we business partners?"

"I helped you grow your business, remember?" he said rolling his eyes.

"I guess so, and I am grateful for that, but that doesn't mean we are in a relationship."

"Yeah sure," he said. "You are so good at playing 'hard to get.'"

Without him knowing, I began to pack up all of my belongings. I needed to get the hell outta the Valley. And so I devised my next plan—to drive the West Coast solo. After one final inspection on my truck, the mechanic said, "If you're planning to drive thousands of miles in this old truck, you'll need to put about $2,800 dollars of repairs into it."

Buzz kill. I wasn't going to make it the entire stretch of the Pacific Coast Highway, so I decided to just leave the Valley.

I moved to Boise to grow my writing business. This was my moment, my chance, to take off. There was just one problem—that's where Willy lived. I rented a space in a woman's three-bedroom home, built my own website, ordered the book *Copywriting for Dummies*, and had meetings with the mayor in the afternoon. I dressed in my most professional attire and Willy kept meeting people and tossing connections my way. I'd get emails, calls, and DMs from random outdoor companies saying that they'd heard I am a really great writer and they'd like to work with me on their branding. What even is branding? I'd Google it.

Running a freelance business for the first time ever is very feast or famine. You make good money, then you make no money. It's promising and then it's complete and utter failure. I was riding the wave of entrepreneurship, but I was completely depressed. In a dead-end relationship, and feeling trapped inside of it. I needed a man to help me along. Women can't be successful on their own, is what I thought, they need men.

I've heard this saying that states people stay in their crummy lives, dealing with the uncomfortable parts of it, until it gets to be too much discomfort. The bad has to outweigh the good. It has to get to that point, the breaking point. After six months of living in Boise, I reached my breaking point. My bank account had fallen once again, and I decided that if this was my last $800 that I ever had in my life—what would I do with it? If I was going to die when this $800 was used up, what would I want? Where would I go?

Greece. I wanted to go to Greece.

And this time, I wasn't going for some missionary-sort of travel. I was going for pleasure. This was, after all, my last $800. My only plan was to drink the wine, eat the cheese, and meet beautiful dark-skinned Greek god-like men. I'd keep working online, of course, and be like all those beautiful traveling women on Instagram. They look so care-free, with hundreds of "likes" and the ability to manage their own time. I began to study these women, some of them were offering courses like "How to Make Money While Traveling," and "Freelance Freedom." I signed up for a few, and then decided I needed my own inspiration. I needed to build myself an inspiration tree of people who inspired me. I found Gary Vaynerchuck, a fire-ball entrepreneur with a badass attitude, and watched him religiously. I found Elizabeth Gilbert, the author of *Eat Pray Love*, and the one woman whose book I'd read annually. I found Brené Brown, a shame researcher—because I needed to work through a lot of shame. I found Glennon Doyle, a truth teller—because I needed to speak my truth. I listened to Tom Brady and Michael Jordan, for obvious reasons. And I followed Oprah who was interviewing all of them and gathering ideas for what it takes to live an authentic and powerful life.

This was my escape route from Willy, I decided. My new inspiration tree would help me along, and I was going to have the time of my life. I was sure of it.

"I'm leaving Boise," I told Willy, "and I am not coming back."

"Why?" he questioned.

"Because I am not doing well, my business is all over the place and it's reliant upon you. I don't like that. I am going to Greece."

"That is so random, and I will go with you to Greece."

He frantically began searching for plane tickets. It was very tempting, I must say, when you have less than a thousand dollars, to allow this person to pay for your entire trip. But no. I couldn't stay with him to support my dreams. I needed to be on my own and that was final.

"You aren't going with me," I said. "I am going alone."

"If you want," he began, searching for a foothold, "I'll manage your business while you're traveling, if you come back and promise we will be together."

I was disgusted. Breaking point. I said thank you for helping me discover my worth, and now I must go.

Situations like this never fall easily. There were months of attempted connections, and I didn't escape without any ties. He offered to keep my truck and all my things at his place, like a storage unit. I accepted, but felt like it was a scam, just another one of his manipulative tricks.

Before I swept myself away to Greece—I visited Minnesota.

Because who knows how long I'll be in Greece? I planned to work on a vineyard for several months, catch a ferry to another island, and meet a charming enologist. We'd probably ride white horses on the beaches of Santorini and sip wine from his family's winery that dates back to 1888. If all of that was going to happen, I decided I should visit my family first.

My time in Minnesota went very quickly, when three days into my visit—the unexpected happened. A man named Jeremiah, who had previously worked with my father, came to my parents' home. We had never met before, but as soon as his truck pulled up in the driveway and a scruffy, strong man stepped out—I felt fireworks explode between the meeting of our eyes. *Does he feel the same way?* Is this another man-trap? No, I thought, this one's different. He kept stealing glances at me as he walked from room to room helping my dad repair things in the house. I looked away. To get myself out of this situation, I went for an hour-long bike ride. With the sun glistening on the winding Mississippi River that runs right next to the bike path, I biked like a starstruck lover in a *Hallmark* movie. Smiling a light smile in the way of the wind, and feeling like angels were kissing my temples, in pure bliss. It. Was. Finally. Happening. But what do I do now? How do I not mess this one up? This is "The One."

When I finally returned to my parents' house, he was waiting for me. Sitting on the back porch, watching the river flow by, we took turns sharing about our lives.

"I think it's really brave that you're going to Greece alone," he said. "I don't think I could do that."

"Oh," I said, blushing, "thank you, but it's more out of necessity to end the last chapter of my life. I really need to leave, and not just to Oregon—I need to leave the country."

He leaned forward in his chair, took off his baseball cap, and said, "I get that."

A moment of silence brought our eyes together.

"Well," he said, "I gotta get going to my game, but if you want to visit my cabin while you're here, I think you'd really like it out there."

"Your cabin?" I said.

"Yeah, well, it's my house, but it's a cabin on a lake."

Wait a second. My dream man owns a cabin on a lake? What is this? *Disney?* He was athletic, funny, charming, and single (well, divorced... but still, single).

IT'S ALL GREEK TO ME

It really wasn't a big deal at the beginning. That is, until my mother asked about his honeymoon. Jeremiah had only been out of the country one time—to some island getaway—for his honeymoon. I tried my best to block out the images of his blonde and athletic ex-wife laying on a beach with him at some all-inclusive resort. She happened to be a graduate from the same high school as me, but we were opposites. I remembered her name being on the front page of the paper always related to sports. Why, I wondered, didn't their marriage work out? They seemed perfect for each other.

I decided to block out my insecurities and visit him at his dreamy cabin home.

After three rosy-cheeked days, we started planning our lives together. Lying in bed one morning, he closed one eye and held up a hand parting his closet at the halfway mark and said, "How about that side of the closet is yours?"

We made plans to get the rest of my belongings from Idaho, but only after Greece. I still had to go to Greece. It was a spiritual rite of passage. I committed to four weeks in Greece instead of forever. I started writing blog posts like the one that I read about being *25 and lost*. I was now twenty-six years old. I had learned so much, and the desperate heartbreaks of my twenties were officially over. I could finally encourage my younger peers, with honesty, that it will get better. You will meet "The One."

Jeremiah and I met in the middle of the summer, and talked seriously about getting married in the fall—there was just one problem: I had to get over his first marriage. It shouldn't be a big hurdle, I told myself, he is in love with me and their relationship is in the past.

And then a tiny, invisible, gnawing, taunting, hateful, jealous green monster hopped on my shoulder and whispered, "you'll never be as important as her," and "he will always be in love with her," and "she is sporty, you're not," and on and on and on. I flicked it off my shoulder time and time again. The first crack that turned into a large spideringweb of pain was this one thought: *maybe there's some truth to this little monster?*

"Why did your marriage end?" I asked him one evening.

"She was a drunk," he said, "and I really didn't ever want to marry her. I hated that day; it was the worst decision of my life."

Not what I expected; I expected some sort of softness towards the first woman he committed his entire life to, so I pressed on.

"You don't need to pretend like you didn't love your first wife," I said. "You're telling me that you *married* someone without being in love with them? Why would you do that?"

"Because I was stressed out and felt like I didn't have any time left to find another person. I settled, okay?"

The green monster gripped its claws into my shoulder and fed machine-gun blows to my ears coercing me to find the *real* story. Find evidence. And then, once again, I shrugged the monster off my shoulder and chose him over the questions. I landed on the fact that he is human, we all make mistakes, and I had to find a way to let it go.

The last days of summer trickled by, and it was time for me go to Greece. Jeremiah brought me to the airport, and all of me wanted to just cancel the trip. I found what I wanted—why did I have to leave the country again? With my bulging backpack, I stepped into the airport with whizzing carts, kids, and people going every which way. Maybe I just... turn around? But he was gone.

I tightened the straps on my backpack and walked through security like the confident woman I was trying to be. From an oval airplane windowpane, I watched the flat ground of Minnesota turn into clouds. Once again, 30,000 feet up in the air and processing my most challenging emotions about myself and my life. I listened to music that reminded me of Jeremiah's arms being wrapped around me and fell asleep to the gentle hum of the airplane's jets taking me far, far from the exact place that I wanted to be. *But this was Greece!* I needed to snap myself out of this lovestruck temper, and fast, because I was about to land in stunning, astonishing, historic, romantic, lovely, magical, deliciously perfect Greece.

Here's the thing about traveling in Greece—if you don't know Greek you better find English speaking friends *real quick*, because the languages are nothing alike. I could get around in other places, say Peru, for example, because they spoke Spanish and that's really not too far from

English. The phrase, "It's all Greek to me," was an honest truth at this point.

My driver didn't speak English too well. His name was Ivan, and Ivan was gray-haired and had many teeth missing. He was a proud man to be taking me to Athens, and we discovered our own style of sign language to get to Athens.

"Greece," he'd say, and fan his arms out across the dusty dash with cigarette butts in the center console, pointing to the ancient buildings we drove past. "Beautiful Greece."

"Yes," I said, looking out over the expansive depth of Greece. "It is beautiful."

"American?" he asked, with raised, long, bushy eyebrows.

"Yep!" I said.

He looked as if I were the president himself visiting, so amped and excited to be seeing an American. He threw a thumbs up and nodded his head in approval very aggressively.

As the sun was setting, he took one turn, and another turn, and then another turn down a brick alleyway and pointed to a red door and said, "There."

"This is it?" I asked. "Through the red door?"

I could tell he didn't register those words, so he just nodded his head and then I got out. With my heart pounding, I decided in that moment I should book safer stays for myself, especially the first night. Walking in through the entrance, I saw a young woman sitting behind the counter.

"Welcome," she said, "To the Backpackers' Hostel at the Red."

"Thank you," I said.

I gave her my name, and she couldn't find me anywhere in their reservations.

"I'm sorry," she said, "Can I see your reservation?"

I pulled out my phone and showed her, to which she responded, "You're at the wrong hostel."

Wrong Hostel

Okay, now I really feel unsafe. I'm in the middle of a country I know nothing about and cannot speak the language, at night, and I don't know where I'm going.

"What?" I said, nervously. "Where is my hostel?"

"This happens often because we are the Backpackers' Hostel *at the Red*," she said. "They're just the Backpackers' Hostel."

Dirty move, I thought. Wow, what a dirty move.

"Okay," I said, taking a deep breath. "How do I get to just the plain old Backpackers' Hostel?"

The lady took out a piece of paper and drew a map for me. It was only a few blocks away, she said. I'd have to deploy my wilderness wayfinding skills once again. I took the map, followed it religiously, and finally arrived at the plain old Backpackers' Hostel. Which, truth be told, wasn't as nice as the one *at the Red*.

But it's Greece, and my four-bed dorm overlooked the sleepless city of Athens. It was dreamy, even if a little dirty and smashed together. The first girl I met was from Romania, her name was Liliana. What is it with these women from countries like Romania? They all seem to be walking sex symbols. I woke up to her walking in at four o'clock in the morning wearing a lacy red tank top, tight high-waisted dark jeans, red heels, and somehow, still, perfect makeup. She wasn't expecting me to be in there, apparently, because she flicked the light on without hesitation. I moved around.

"Oh my God!" she yelled. "You scared me; sorry I turned the light on."

She flicked the light off and fell asleep in, I kid you not, under thirty seconds, still wearing her nightlife getup. Heels and all. When I woke up, she was still dead asleep, not even a slight movement. I made some coffee and sat out on the balcony, thinking about Jeremiah. What would it be like if he were here? Could we travel together? He was very "country," and I was very "free-spirited traveler." I wasn't sure if I wanted him to be traveling with me in Greece, or traveling with me at all.

Traveling was something that I did, alone.

Eventually, Liliana came walking out onto the balcony wearing a cream-colored silky robe. It was so thin I could see her lacy bra and thong underneath. I was wearing athletic shorts and an oversized jersey.

"Good morning darling," she said. "I'm so sorry for coming in late last night. I met just the most wonderful people on a rooftop bar. Where are you from?"

I desperately wished I was wearing a mid-century corset with fishnet tights, naturally, at nine thirty in the morning, and could inform her that I was actually a local.

"I'm from the States," I said, instead.

"Oh! I love New York."

I decided to just roll with it. "Yes," I said. "The city of dreams!"

"What brings you to Greece?"

"Just travel," I said. "I'm kind of having a hard time though because I met the man I want to marry right before leaving."

"Oh," she said. "I understand that," and held up her phone displaying her (a model) and some guy that wasn't half as gorgeous as her and said, "This is the man I want to marry."

And then she kept going, "But he has cheated on me several times, and it hasn't been a fairytale, you know. We're working things out."

I wanted to say *cheat??* On YOU? Have you seen yourself and what is wrong with this dude? Instead, I told her I'm sorry to hear about that and I shouldn't be giving her advice, but she should find someone who will be faithful to her.

"I am so insecure about myself and I get really clingy to him and..." she shared, lightly caressing the contour of her collarbone, "I just get so addicted to his approval of me and I can't let him go."

"Hm," I said. "That's really crazy to hear because you're seriously gorgeous."

"Thank you," she said, looking shy and seductive at the same time. "But hey, I gotta go, I'm meeting him at the ferry station in an hour."

"Your ex?" I said. "Or whatever he is?"

"Yes, he is my boyfriend."

And then she was gone, and it was me, myself, and Athens.

What Did You Really Come to Greece For?

I took myself out on the town, in Athens, to feel the energy of ancient history. Walking around on the cobblestone streets of Athens felt like *wearing* philosophy. The only problem was that it was the middle of August and hotter than hot outside. I rented a bike and had to stop at a corner store to buy salted almonds and water, so I didn't pass out from a heat stroke. When I went to return the bike, I met a blonde guy about my age from the Netherlands. He was working at the hotel adjacent to my hostel. Not a smashed-in backpackers' hostel, but a state-of-the-art Greek hotel with marble lobby floors. His name was Camden. And Camden, I don't know why he decided to do this, offered me an invitation.

"Say," he said, in a very polite accent, "would you like to sit in our rooftop pool?"

I'd only sweat out seventeen gallons of water biking around the blazing hot city for the last three hours. I must've looked like a distressed lonely female.

"Are you serious?" I said. "No, I can't, I am not staying here. I was only renting the bikes."

"It doesn't matter," he said. "Where you stay?"

I pointed to the hostel.

"No problem. Grab swimwear and meet me by the elevator."

I tried to act cool about this, but I was *sprinting* to get my swimsuit as soon as I was out of his eyesight. When I returned, he was waiting for me, in his white button up, navy blue pants with a brown belt and perfect brown dress shoes.

In the glass elevator headed to the top floor, he gave me the rundown, "If anybody asks, you say you know Vince," he said, "Okay?"

"Vince," I repeated. "Does Vince have a last name or?"

"Just Vince."

"Got it."

The elevator opened to a sea of women in string bikinis with their tan, tattooed, and muscular boyfriends lounging about. I was wearing a knitted sage-colored swimsuit I bought from Target two years ago that desperately needed replacing. Pulling out my novel, I tried my best to quietly shrink into the background of this hip hop music video I'd just been placed in, but felt massively out of place. The models took turns swimming to the edge of the pool, which overlooked all of Athens, and their boyfriends captured sexy-hot photos of them arching their booties out of the water and looking out at the restless city. One girl took her long acrylic fingernails and strung the lines of her bikini up around her hips to wedge the little triangle of fabric up into her butt cheeks. I couldn't help it; I laughed a quiet, restrained laugh. The *Sports Illustrated* model spun around and glared at me. I covered my mouth and focused back on my novel.

When I decided I'd used up all of my free time in the pool, I went back down to see Camden smiling. "How was it?"

"It was perfect," I said. "Absolutely perfect, thank you."

And then I left. He watched me leave, and I know this, because I turned around right before the big glass doors automatically opened and glanced at him one last time. He didn't turn away, he just kept watching me.

I took myself out to dinner that night, in the glow of the candlelit side street cafés. This is where I met my first true seductive Greek man. I'd met a seductive Romanian woman, a semi-seductive Netherlandic man, and now, for the real thing—the Greek man. He was the waiter but definitely not afraid to approach women on the job; it seemed to be a part of his job.

"You dine alone, love?"

"Yes," I said. "Just me and the city!"

"You have no boyfriend?" he asked, looking up and down the street.

"I do have a boyfriend," I said, showing him the background photo on my phone of Jeremiah and me.

"Ah," he said, "but he isn't here. So tonight, you are single."

"Not exactly," I said. "I am still in a relationship and I want to marry him."

He didn't look convinced.

"Then why you come to Greece?" he questioned. "Alone?"

"I like to travel."

"But what did you *really* come to Greece for?"

Point taken. He was right. I came to Greece for the cheese, the wine, and sex with men that would probably be a lot like him. But now, it was all different. I no longer wanted my wild free days, I wanted commitment. I? Me? Wanted commitment? What was happening to me?

Three Solo Women, Traveling Together

I had booked my one-way ticket to Greece alone, and by the time the trip arrived—I was no longer alone. One of my best friends, Megan, decided to join me on a whim. And with her came another woman named Patricia, whom she'd met on her travels to the hostel. The three of us traveled to the first island, Santorini, together. Patricia traveled in luxury, while Megan and I were more like the sleep-on-the-floor type people. But once you have luxury, you crave luxury.

We booked a stay at the same cottage as Patricia, where it was Honeymooners' Central. Starry-eyed couples were all over the place, ladies all spoken for and proud to be wearing so much white. White swimsuits, white sundresses, white evening dresses, white bags, fresh white diamonds on their hands and necks. We were anything but all white. For starters, my backpack that I traveled with was bright yellow like a warning signal. Patricia preferred to travel in black, she'd been through the throes of a nasty divorce. Black looked good on Patricia, though, she didn't look sad and divorced, she looked sexy, single, and powerful. And Megan? She was all of the wilderness in a woman— sporting a teal dress, pine-colored backpack, and sandals that looked like Jesus himself had worn them.

Our cottage was also all-white, with stucco walls, a floor-to-ceiling glass shower complete with a rainfall showerhead, and tiles that were white and blue. We had a balcony that overlooked the pool, where all the newlywedded ladies were floating with their suntan lotions and giving their new husbands drink demands. Once again, sitting in an antique white chair on a balcony in Santorini, my mind wandered to Jeremiah. *Where was he? What was he doing? Was he thinking of me?*

"I'm gonna go get a drink," Megan said. "You coming?"

"Yeah," I said. "I wanna get in that pool, with my drink."

The three of us lounged around reading our books, talking about men currently in our lives and men whose time had expired in our lives, while sipping drinks all afternoon well into the evening. Even though I missed Jeremiah, sorely, I couldn't pinpoint why I didn't really wish that he were accompanying me instead of these two women. I liked us, three solo women traveling together. Perhaps it's the empowerment of being alone? Or maybe, it was deeper? Was I afraid to get married? Just as much as I missed Jeremiah, I also thought about his past marriage. The two came together, in equal parts. Missing him and ruminating on their marriage.

Megan and I went on to visit the islands of Crete and Agistri. Crete is the largest island, and Agistri is one of the smallest. After the taste of luxury that we got from spending a night with Patricia, who had continued on her solo travels to another island, we stayed in nicer Airbnbs and hotels on both islands. Spending time with Megan, I began to realize, was just so easy. I didn't have to worry if she was enjoying herself or that she was occupied. Some days we spent doing our own thing, exploring around the island. And others, like her final day, we spent well thought-out and planned.

"I have a few things I'd like to do on my final day in Greece," Megan said at dinner, where we shared a glass pitcher of wine the night before. "I want to swim in the ocean naked, bike around the island, and eat Greek yogurt."

And that's exactly what we did. We biked until we found a semi-hidden part of the island, and then we stripped down and walked into the crystalline-aqua waters of the Aegean Sea. We floated atop the water's surface, boobies popping out of the water like white chocolate Hershey's kisses. Life, in that moment, could not have gotten any better.

ONE LAST ISLAND

After Megan left, I had one more island to go—the Island of Skopelos. This island was quite possibly the most important one because my favorite movie, *Mamma Mia*, was filmed there. And I was, once again, not alone but this time with my mother.

In the movie *Mamma Mia*, Meryl Streep is "Donna Sheridan" who plays the mother of the bride. My mother and I had watched this movie many, many times, and memorized all the sing-along ABBA songs and dances. The daughter, played by Amanda Seyfried, is named "Sophie." Sophie gets married on the island of Skopelos in the Church of Agios Ioannis Kastri. The church sits on top of a narrow path that leads up 223 steps carved into a barren rock that juts out of the sea like a great frozen wave that turned to stone. My mother and I walked each of the steps, pretending to be Meryl Streep singing *The Winner Takes It All*.

Though the church was a dream, the island paradise, and the endless supply of delicious feta cheese, bread, and wine was nothing short of luxurious—I still craved being with Jeremiah on that seaweed-infested northern Minnesota lake in a log cabin. *Isn't this something*, I thought while sitting in an open windowsill overlooking Skopelos, *I have all this and all I want is him*?

The host of the room my mother and I rented was a doll, a vivacious woman in her fifties whose energy reflected that of a twenty-two-year-old. We had afternoon wine with her, and she asked about my love life, of course. It seemed to be the question that Greeks unashamedly led with: *Are you married? If not, when are you getting married?*

I told the woman that no I am not married, but my mother added that I would likely soon be engaged. We all knew I had met "The One," and it was such a lovely family story. Two individuals, who didn't know the other one existed, met one midsummer afternoon and fell madly in love.

"Take a pamphlet," the woman said, "I'll give you and your wedding party a discount if you'd like to get married here in Greece."

"That would be a dream," I said, accepting the small beautifully-designed pamphlet.

Getting married in Greece? Dreams really do come true. My mother and I spent our final hours on the island of Skopelos dreaming of my wedding, though also talking about Jeremiah's first wedding. Because, ya know, my parents were there, at his first wedding.

"She wasn't the right one," my mother consoled me. "It was a mistake."

"But why did it happen?" I questioned.

"People make mistakes all the time. Unfortunately, his was a marriage."

I wanted to buy it, but something got stuck deep inside of me that I couldn't rid from my core. What was it? Jealously? Fear? Resentment? I couldn't pinpoint the issue, but all I knew is that I had to get his ex out of my mind so I could be with him. And fast. Because when I returned to Minnesota, we were to begin planning our wedding.

BLOCKING IT OUT

There was just one problem: the more I tried to block it out, the worse it got. I kept it quiet upon my arrival back to Minnesota and into my lover's arms at last. *There*, I thought, *I'd made it home and this is where I belong.* I can let the past go now. Except there wasn't just the issue of me being afraid of his past marriage, he was also afraid that I'd leave him. *All the other women left, why wouldn't I?*

And that was his logic. It was somewhat comforting to know that I wasn't the only person in this relationship with insecurities. Though his comment only deepened the wound I felt for his past marriage. If she left him, did that mean he wanted to stay? Jeremiah and I spent our days in each other's arms, staring deeply into each other's eyes and making a plan to recover my things from Idaho and make our lives final together. This would mean all ties that Willy had to me would finally be cut loose. He wasn't willing to let go easily, however. While making plans to fly out to Idaho, stay with a friend, and gather my belongings, Willy thought that was just too informal.

"I'll come get you from the airport," he insisted. "It's not a problem, and you can stay here with me."

Of course, I couldn't tell him that Jeremiah was coming with me—that would be a sight I didn't want to see, nor anybody else. He believed I was traveling solo, just to gather my things. After several FaceTime calls, I requested that he doesn't call me anymore—just text me for what's necessary. *Leave a key under the mat and I'll collect my things and be on my way, and thank you for taking care of them.* A thought flashed through my mind, *what if he has destroyed them all?* I prayed for the best and prepared for the worst. And then I received a message that gave me red-hot anger, very near hatred: your truck might not work and I am not leaving a key under the mat.

I messaged back: Why wouldn't my truck work?

Willy: Because I thought the battery should be unplugged while it sat there. I haven't found the time to put it back. I don't know if it will work.

Me: Really?

Willy: I guess we will see if it works.

Me: Why can't you just leave a key under the mat? I will be in and out.

Willy: I need to be there because it's not safe to have the key under a mat. I have kids.

Me: Are the kids there right now?

Willy tries to FaceTime.

I decline.

Me: Dude, just leave a key—for real? Your kids? You can remove the key once I am gone.

Willy: Silence.

My friend who I traveled to South Africa with and had since moved to Boise, Tammy, picked Jeremiah and me up from the airport. She was exactly what I needed: stout and stern.

Jeremiah waited at a hotel, but on call—just in case. Tammy and I prepared to go in, gather my things, and be out of there. She began to prep me on the way, "This is a *mission*. Okay? He is going to try to talk to you all nice. This is not the time. You are done and he needs to understand. Just keep packing and moving. Packing and moving."

I nodded and repeated after her, *packing and moving*, and felt my heart begin to pound in shame for being in this situation, and fear for the fight that could happen.

When we arrived, Willy opened up the front door to his apartment and showed my small section of things sitting in his living room. Thankfully, a traveler never has much to move. It was a just a few bins, climbing gear, and books.

"Here you go," he said, "all of your stuff."

Tammy put her head down and began to muscle boxes out of the apartment and into my truck. I helped, while Willy attempted to make small talk about mutual acquaintances. My truck started just fine, I thanked him, and he began asking if we could talk more. I said no, we need to go. And just like that, in under fifteen minutes, Tammy and I were gone. My body, stiff and filled with anger, began to relax as soon as we made it back to Jeremiah. The travels from Idaho back to Minnesota with Jeremiah were filled with love-lust, future planning, and complete terror that this little wedge of his past marriage would become the thing to break us apart.

It just didn't make sense to me. I had barely been in a serious relationship that lasted more than a year, and had nothing to compare a marriage to. It sounded very serious, the whole marriage thing. Prior to Jeremiah, I could barely step into a relationship, as a *girlfriend*. Jeremiah traveled often for work, and I worked from home on writing contracts, which is never good for a female's wandering brain. If a woman thinks there is evidence to be found, she will sniff it out like a blood hound. I spent the evenings he was away for work searching for evidence that he wasn't quite over his ex-wife. There had to be evidence, somewhere.

What I found I accused him of, such as old tuxedos and notes that mentioned his marriage to her. And then he came home, we cuddled and made love, and all was right in the world once again. Until the next thought, which typically road on the coattails of us planning *our* wedding.

"Don't you think we're moving a little fast?" I said.

"Not if you know," he said. "I'm ready to start a family."

I wore his flannels, went deer hunting, drove his truck, and made him dinner. I cleaned his laundry, went for walks around the lake with his neighbors, and in less than three months—I'd transformed from a traveling gypsy into a rural Minnesotan man's housewife. *I could do this life*, I told myself. It's time for me to settle down, and I'm madly in love with Jeremiah. He is my soulmate. For the first time in my life, I didn't feel like I had to hide my relationship status. I posted photos of us on social media, kept a photo of us as the background on my phone, and started items in my notes such as "wedding songs" and "venues." I was really doing this thing.

Just Get Over It

Months went by and the pressure to get engaged was building. I wanted him to ask me to marry him, but there was this thing I had yet to do—get over his first marriage. It was like this constant radiating, annoying, beeping red light between us. Why couldn't this thing just shut up and go away? I began to seek help. First by calling my friend's parents who were divorced. Then my sisters and my brother. Then I sought counseling, again. I talked and talked to everyone under the sun who would listen to my concerns about marrying a divorced man. Prayer warriors from my church were summoned to pray for me to break the soul ties I had to past men in my life, because the problem wasn't Jeremiah—it was me.

Things started looking up, we were planning our impending engagement, and then a global pandemic swept across the nation called COVID-19. Suddenly, he was no longer traveling for work and we were both working from home. Without space to breathe, like a wound lacking oxygen, our problems began to fester and cause great irritation. Seven months later, I left him for a weekend to stay at my parents' house and process in my brain what was wrong with me. I journaled and prayed. I meditated and had long conversations with my mother, even longer conversations with God. Jeremiah talked with my parents. It was fine, except the spark was slowly going out. The flame that we had so innocently stumbled into existence was quickly diminishing before our eyes—and I was the one putting it out.

Sitting in my childhood bedroom, I wrote down on a piece of paper how I feel about marriage. Maybe the issue wasn't that I couldn't get over *his* marriage, maybe the issue was that I wasn't sure if I wanted to *be* married? Now that concept, I realized, was somewhat reasonable. The idea that I just couldn't get over his ex-wife was so not reasonable. I worked with myself as a mother does with a child trying to convince them to buckle their seatbelt. *This car is not moving until you buckle your seatbelt, kid.* It's just that "forever" wasn't a fifteen-minute car ride from the house to daycare, forever was day-in-and-day-out forever. It felt so *final*, like permanent Sharpie scribbled on a wall. Embroidered towels and signs that have our last name written in cursive that we'd hang in our entryway.

So final. And where does the old gypsy soul of Emilee go? The one who traveled to South Africa alone? And Tanzania? Who built her writing business? Lived out of a truck? Trekked through the desert with angry teenagers? Where did she go, now that she would become a *housewife*? I decided that all women must feel this way when transitioning from "me" to "we" and all my concerns would melt away once I realize I have an attractive, smart, strong, bearded man at my side. I stayed at my parents' house through the weekend when I received sudden news: Jeremiah was in the hospital.

NOT FAMILY

"I had the worst stomach pains in my life," he said. "I didn't know what was happening."

"And why didn't you call me?" I questioned.

"Because what were you going to do? I was in such extreme pain; I had to leave and drive myself to the hospital."

"Okay, just please let me know what the doctor says."

Five hours later, Jeremiah called to inform me his appendix had burst and they removed it. He had to stay in the hospital for the rest of the week. And because of COVID, anyone who wasn't family couldn't visit. *Who wasn't family?*

"I know what you're thinking," he said. "That my ex, because she was my wife at one point, could've visited me, but you can't."

I wanted to deny the thought, but it was a thought.

"That did cross my mind," I said.

"You gotta get over this, it's literally killing me. I am in the hospital because of you. YOU are causing me all of this stress because you won't just let it go."

I began to cry, hysterically. It was all my fault. I had serious brain issues. Why couldn't I just allow myself to be happy? My parents came with me a week later to pick him up from the hospital. We sat in the car in silence, with him being overly respectful to my parents and overly silent with me.

"I'm here, Jeremiah, I'm trying."

"Not hard enough," he said.

To care for him post-surgery, I moved back into his house. He barely moved and I became his 24/7 nurse, refilling water bottles, giving him meds, making food when he could eventually eat, ushering in guests to visit him, and sleeping on a cot beside him as he slept on the couch to remain in an upright position. The pandemic, however, made a lot of the world realize that if you jam two people inside a home that are already having issues, the issues are likely to get worse—not better. Though my lovesick heart wanted to believe the opposite.

"This isn't working," he said one morning, "We need to be done. I'm calling someone else to come take care of me. I don't want you here anymore."

My heart sank.

"Please don't do this," I said. "I am here and I'm not leaving you. I want to take care of you. I want to show you that I can get over it and I am."

"You won't ever get over it."

"I don't even bring it up anymore," I said. "How can you say that I'm not over it? Only I get to decide that."

"Because," he snickered, "you're never going to."

Waiting During an Emergency

As the days went by and Jeremiah healed physically, he got angrier with me as a person. We attempted to go for a four-wheeler ride, which we used to enjoy together, and instead he pulled on my arms and told me I was driving it wrong. I was going to crash his four-wheeler. Did I not care about anything? This was *his* property, not mine. And do you *try* to leave drops of coffee on the counter every time you pour yourself a cup? And the dirt? Do you just trail dirt in from the front yard for fun? Hoping I'll clean it up?

I finally decided to take space, so I left for a weekend at my sister's place in Minneapolis. Once again, time apart. I was hanging on every word he said, and desperately hoping he would call me to apologize for the way he was speaking to me—but he never did. I spent the weekend at my sister's house, without sleep, rocking back and forth in pain over the fact that this relationship was soon going to be over. She also worked from home and was taking clients for health coaching on the side. That night, she had one client meeting for an hour, and I called TJ to be on the phone with me because I was afraid to be alone for an hour. I feared I'd make the plan (they always ask if you've made a plan) and follow through on it. It was no longer safe for me to care for myself. I needed surveillance.

"If you love him," my friend consoled me over the phone, "then you've got to make it work. Drive out there and tell him how much you love him."

"Okay," I said. "I can do that."

I drove out to his house imagining we'd heal this entire thing, and be in love once again. He would pick me up, tell me how much he loves me, and forgive me for my messed-up thought patterns. We might even decide to get married right then and there—go to the courthouse and not make a big deal about it. However, when I arrived at his house, heart-pounding, he was not there.

I walked into the house to find sweet alcoholic drinks I'd never even thought of purchasing or trying, and the house a complete mess. Blankets everywhere, all my things smashed in drawers and hidden. It was as if I suddenly didn't know the man that I was in love with, or the man that lived here wasn't him.

Days turned into weeks and our communication diminished, my confidence and love for myself right along with it. *How could I have messed this one up?* It was the perfect set-up, and somehow, I managed to make this man have complete contempt and hatred for me. I didn't sleep or eat, and when I did eat, I threw up. I shook with terror, waiting for him to reach out and tell me that it would all be okay. Except that day never came. I had moved into my parents' house with a duffle bag of clothes, and soon, I needed to gather more of my things. I called Jeremiah, and he was stern, with anger in his voice, telling me that I needed to get all of my stuff out of his house within the week—otherwise he was going to throw it all out.

I was not only heartbroken but shocked. How could a man who wanted to marry me a few months ago now completely kick me out of his life? *This is not happening. This is not happening. This is not happening.* I repeated that to myself, but the worst most awful part about it all was that it was happening. I had lost twenty pounds and found a moment of happiness when I tried on my Hollister jeans from high school, size four, and they fit. My body, however, on the inside was like a crumbling, leaking building that was sold to a new owner and they decided to bulldoze the entire thing down to the ground. Too much to fix in that one—just let it crumble to the ground and build something new.

During this time, I began biking a lot. I went on hours-long bike rides, listening to music with messages like "we're all broken," and "we all make mistakes," and "run free bird, sing free, be yourself," you know, messages trying to remind myself that other people have gone through awful things too and maybe there was a way through. Now that I was living at my parents' house, I sat in my childhood bedroom, overlooking the driveway and open field that leads to the Mississippi River, and wished I could just go back to innocence. Before I knew what intense, sickening heartbreak and loss felt like. Before I had to act like an adult. I was now working for one of the most widely recognized magazines in the state of Minnesota, as editor-in-chief. It was the position I had dreamed I'd one day have, and I got it much earlier in life than I had imagined. There was just one problem—I was barely standing on my own. Living in my childhood bedroom, heartbroken, and feeling like I'd not only let myself down, but my family as well. They wanted Jeremiah to be my husband, and I was finally going to do something normal in life. I was finally going to fit in. I would have the house, the career, the husband, and we'd probably get a dog. All of that was gone now, and I was here—alone, once again.

One afternoon, I was sitting at my white rickety desk in my room, working on the fall issue of the magazine, when I suddenly had extremely bad stomach pains. I writhed over in pain, and wondered if my body was actually going into starvation mode. I could barely stand up. As I pressed on my stomach, I noticed it was on the lower right abdomen. *What if my body is mirroring what Jeremiah went through? What if I have appendicitis?* It was an intense, awful pain, and then it was gone. I went downstairs to find my mother, and she said we should call. I called the doctor's office, and a nurse told me I should allow an ambulance to come get me and go straight to the emergency room. This shocked me even more, I thought she'd tell me to take a few TUMS and drink some water. I didn't want to be brought in by ambulance, so my mother drove me. Fast. Screaming fast, while I held my stomach, and wondered if Jeremiah found out I was in the hospital, would he care?

When we made it to the emergency room, there was a wait.

As I sat in the waiting room, I thought this was kind of odd. Waiting during an emergency. When they brought me back, they ran a whole gamut of tests. Blood tests, CAT scans, urine tests, ultrasound tests, they just kept coming. Four hours later, the nurse came walking in and said they haven't found anything besides cysts on my ovaries. Polycystic Ovary Syndrome. PCOS. This was nothing new to me, I've had that since high school. It basically just made me have off-set periods and wonder if I could ever have kids. I accepted both, took a drug called Metformin to help regulate my period, and life surely moved right along after that diagnosis.

I stared at the nurse. "So, my appendix is fine?" I said.

"Yes, you might want to just watch it, but it seems to be fine."

I wasn't sure how one keeps watch on their appendix, but I was sure I'd figure that part out as well. Leaving the hospital, I felt like the whole emergency run was not necessary at all—but I was grateful that I had insurance. Until, of course, the bill came. I owed $8,080 for all of the tests rendered. This cannot be, I thought, I have insurance? I called the insurance company and they said, "it looks like they didn't find anything new, so we are not able to cover this bill." I broke out in an all-out sweat, from head to toe. I screamed, loudly, and walked outside. My parents ran outside to see me circling and crying, literally wishing there was a door that would appear, and I could walk into it and pass away into afterlife.

My mother yelled to my father, "You need to hold her, she is not stable!"

Dad walked out onto the blacktop tar, where TJ and I parked our cars in high school without a care in the world, just basketball practice and good music; where boys snuck over in the middle of the night to hang out with my friends and me; where we finished runs and played games; and now where my father just held me repeating the words, "It's only money. We will figure this out. It's only money."

Yes, it's only money, but $8,080 was twice as much as I had in my bank account at the time. How was I going to pay this bill? I applied for financial assistance from the hospital, knowing that this was my Hail Mary. When the letter of rejection came two weeks later, I felt the hot-flash-life-is-over sweat once again and decided to go on a long bike ride. The leaves were transforming at the beginning months of fall, and I began to soften as I pedaled along this quiet forested path. It would be okay, I told myself. It would, somehow, work out. I didn't know how, but maybe all this was going to make me stronger? I am becoming a warrior. About six miles into the bike ride, my tire went flat. That was it, this had gone too far, and I didn't know why the Universe or God or some unseen controlling force hated me.

I walked another two miles to a park, sat down on the curb, and balled. I let my head fall into my hands, my knees fall in toward each other, and my entire sad building of a frame closed in on itself. There was nobody else around, until a van pulled up. A van of rough looking men. *Great*, I thought, *now I'm going to get gang-banged in real life*. Awesome. The van stopped in front of me abruptly, and one very muscular man with tattoos and a large cross necklace came walking out looking directly at me. Another skinny, dark-haired man with a lot of piercings came walking out next. And then a short, stout, rough-looking man. I was terrified. My eyes were probably all big and wide as I was trying to decide if I could outrun them (I couldn't).

The first guy with the tattoos held his hand out like one does to a traumatized dog. "It's okay," he said. "I just saw you crying and asked that we stop to help you. Are you okay?"

"Oh," I said, relaxing a little bit, "I'm just having the worst day of my life and my tire popped on the way here."

He put my bike up on this frame and began to look at it. There was a pump at the park, and he began to pump fiercely. Just kept pumping and pumping like his life depended on it. Another man came walking out and said, "T, man, I don't think that bike is gonna hold air, the whole tire gotta be replaced."

I don't know what his real name was, but apparently, they called him "T."

"It's fine," I said. "I can call my father."

"Sorry we couldn't help with your bike," T said. "But can we pray for you?"

I began to tear up, and said yes.

More men climbed out of the van, there were about twelve of them, and they all circled around me, placing hands on my shoulders, and on each other's shoulders, and T began to pray. "God," he said, "I don't know what is happening in our sister's life right now, but You know. I pray that You give her the strength to make it through this hard time, and she is reminded that she is so loved by You. She is seen and recognized as a daughter of the King." After he said these words, he just stood there, hands on my shoulders, silent.

"That was so sweet," I said through drips of tears, "You guys just made my day. Where are you from?"

T responded, "Minnesota Adult and Teen Challenge."

A recovery home for addicts. This made me cry even more, because these men had gone through a lot of loss in their lives. They had landed themselves in a ninety-day treatment facility, trying to move forward with their lives from drug and alcohol addictions—and here they were—praying for a girl with a broken heart.

I thanked them, and they were on their way once again. I decided that I would hold onto the tiny little beautiful moments like that one. Even through all the pain and frustration, moments such as these made me question: *Maybe God is real and with me?*

YOU CAN'T LEAVE ME

Four months later, I ran into a friend of Jeremiah's at the gym. He was meant to be the best man at our wedding. I had been avoiding him because I thought he must think I am a terribly messed up person because I couldn't allow myself to marry Jeremiah and get over his past marriage. I couldn't just allow the process; I had to make everything so damn challenging. I thought he'd avoid me too, but this time he walked directly up to me. I began to sweat.

"Hey, how are you?" he asked.

This was surprising to me. He was asking how I was doing.

"I'm okay," I said. "Still hurting, bad. I don't think another person will ever hurt me as much as he has."

"You'll move on," he said, "you're young and beautiful."

So, that's it? I wondered. *My pain doesn't matter because I'm young and beautiful?* He continued, "Can you believe that Jeremiah invited me to his wedding?"

"Excuse me?"

"Yeah, you didn't know he is engaged?" he said.

More shock. "No, I had no idea," I said. "Wow, that was fast, just shy of six months."

This was a lot to process—I walked away, trying to appear as though I wouldn't faint, and went straight to the yoga room. I cried no more tears that day and decided I needed to get away for a little while. I had to leave, but where would I go? I called my brother.

"Em," TJ said in the most calming tone, "you'll fall in love again. It's just hard right now."

"No, Teej, I was one thousand percent sure that it was him, I will never love someone again, and I've completely messed up my entire life."

"That's not possible. You didn't mess up, and you will make it through this," he said.

"Can I come stay with you?"

"Of course," he said.

When I arrived at my brother's apartment in Minneapolis, he dropped everything to spend the weekend with me. We biked twenty-three miles with a speaker strapped to his bike shamelessly playing Taylor Swift on shuffle. His girlfriend surprised us with a painting class, where we drank wine and made beautiful sunsets on canvas. We went out for dinner, just the two of us. Sitting in a downtown Irish pub, I told him how badly I was hurting.

"I'm really not okay," I said. "It's like I'm continually falling, and there's no landing spot. I just keep falling and falling. This is the worst pain of my life. I think it has cut a real hole in my stomach."

He didn't know what to say, I could tell. *What does one say to that?* But he was doing his best to just be present. Sometimes, when loved ones go through hard times, we feel like we must say something magical or perfect to get them through—when most often, just being there is enough.

I told him that for the first time in my life, I wanted to choose the "out." Only a human who doesn't deserve to be here could mess up the perfect set-up to have the American dream of a life. I had botched it. And now, with my heart still attached to Jeremiah and him happily waltzing off into the sunset with his new fiancé, I figured the best option for me would be to escape from the pain. To disappear off the face of the planet and become dirt once again.

TJ didn't say a lot that day, but on the drive back to his place, he began to tear up. I was surprised by this because I don't think I had ever seen my brother tear up before. With a quivering lip, he said, "Em, I know it's hard right now, but you can't leave me. I need you here."

This made me tear up, which I had done a lot of, and was surprised that my eyes could still make tears. If I meant this much to TJ, the one person on the planet that I looked up to as if he were a celebrity, then I had to find a way through it all. I had to keep fighting, for him.

Weeks turned into months, and still, the pain did not lessen. But I was there—fighting. My parents rented a condo in Florida that winter, and I told them I wasn't going. The year prior, I had visited the same place, and Jeremiah was with me. Now, I was alone, and would have to travel there without him. I was hoping that TJ would go, because that would make me want to go. TJ was the center of most travel decisions that I made, and the same in reverse. Every Christmas, when I lived in Idaho, I'd get a call: *Em, you gonna be home for Christmas? Or Easter?* The chances of either of us attending anything went up by large percentages if the other person was attending. Our trips in high school during spring break were the most epic, the two of us meeting large groups of friends and spending our days feeling like a dream-team on the beach. Rippin' it up on jet skis, smashin' people in beach volleyball games, ziplining over jungle canopies, drinking too many daiquiris and dancing in cages in downtown bars (well, me, I drank too many daiquiris and danced in the cages, he had better discipline). TJ was the center of all the energy, he was the party-starter, the party-keeper-goer, the person everyone wanted on their team.

I needed him to join me in Florida, so I could laugh on the beach with him and maybe smack a team or two in beach volleyball just like we used to do. Instead, I got a call from my mother asking me to check in with my brother because he said he wasn't going to Florida. *There's something not right here*, I thought, TJ would take any opportunity to be oceanside that he could. He *lived* in Florida at one point for God's sake.

I FaceTimed him.

"Sup, Em?" he answered, sitting on his couch with his hood up.

"Why you not going to Florida?"

"I don't know, I am just stressed with work and all that, don't feel like going, I guess."

There was no convincing him. I knew it. So, I decided I wouldn't go either until my sister convinced me to travel with her. My middle sister, Anna, is the life coach of the bunch. She is a real, certified life coach, and I was recently her most challenging client. Because at this point, I had moved into her house, just a few miles away from my parents, to try my best to get my independent shaky legs under me again. Day in and day out, she found me crumpled on the floor beside my desk in a heap of tears, and she took a moment to sit on the floor with me. To pray with me. To pick an oil, rub it on my palms, and read a healing verse we found in a book titled *Essential Oils and Emotions*. While I wasn't an actual paying "client" of hers during that time, she never treated me as a burden. She took me into her space, held me with grace, and gave me room to cry, to scream, to talk all about how I'd ruined my life forever, and then she said in the most calming way that all of this would change if I just trust in the process and journey. She reminded me of the differences that Jeremiah and I had and asked if I truly wanted to be a housewife in northern Minnesota with babies and boiling stews while Jeremiah worked on the road.

While sitting on the first plane to Florida, I put on a hoodie and listened to music that probably didn't make me feel any better. I was so riddled with anxiety and heartbreak that I thought I might throw up, again. An acidy feeling started rising in my stomach, so I crawled over two people and walk-sprinted to the bathroom. I threw up once on that flight and once on the second flight.

But I was fighting. I was still fighting.

When we arrived at my parents' condo, I spent two days sitting out on the balcony watching the sun rise and the sun set, the ocean wash in and the ocean wash out, people playing and people lounging. Everything was telling me that life goes on, but I wasn't ready for it yet. I was still in therapy and met with my counselor, who was like having a gay best friend, and he reprimanded me for going to therapy while I was near the ocean.

"Why didn't you just cancel your therapy appointment and enjoy being there, honey?" he asked.

"Because, I can't just enjoy being here. *I am heartbroken!* I can't process anything."

We talked in-depth about our relationship dynamics. He gave me a perspective about Jeremiah that I had never processed myself. He was certain our relationship never would've worked. I would constantly be trying to free myself, and he would constantly be trying to control me. He said that I had dodged a bullet and to enjoy being in Florida. That phrase "dodged a bullet" was one that I'd hear not only from this therapist, but from my next two therapists as well, as I kept changing counselors to find the one who could figure out what was wrong with me. If they shined the light on him, I'd knock them sideways to remove the blame from him and place the blazing, burning white-hot shame back on me where it belonged.

My therapists began using this term I'd never heard before called "narcissism." It sounded like love-bombing, control, and the cyclical nature of chaos. I thought that really sounded like our relationship, but I figured I must be the narcissist. So, I took a narcissist test and scored a big fat 0 out of 10 and figured then, still not convinced, that the test mustn't be running properly. The last line in my results read, "the fact that you're even taking this test proves you not to be a narcissist." I couldn't figure it out, so I stayed in therapy like a life raft, barely keeping my head above water, taking large gasps of air, and then dunking myself again under the all-consuming waves of shame, blame, and jealously.

After our session, I thanked him and then walked out of my parents' condo and to the entrance of the elevator. Standing there, before I even pressed the button, I made a pact with myself, verbalized out loud, that went something like this: *As soon as this here elevator door opens, you have fifteen floors to return to happy and free Emilee once again. That's it. You cannot hold this pain any longer. It is physically impossible. And so, this is your ceremonial release. This is your wedding back home to yourself. This is where you find your gypsy freedom once again. Fifteen floors toward freedom.*

Barefoot, in a white one-piece swimsuit and a Turkish shawl wrapped lightly around my shoulders, I got into the elevator. Thankfully, there was no one else in the elevator because if there was, they would now be a part of my ceremony home to myself whether they liked it or not. I held my hands over my heart and repeated, *I'm coming home to me, happy free Emilee. I'm coming home to me, happy free Emilee.* For fifteen whole uninterrupted floors I repeated that same phrase with eyes closed and the smallest, slightest little sliver of peace rising within me. When it landed on the first floor, I walked right past the pool where kids were splashing, and parents were chatting. I walked right past the bar and the shaved ice machine. I walked onto the hot sand and past the people lounging on laid-back chairs. I walked past women lying on towels with their sun tan lotions and novels. Past yesterday's besieged sandcastles. As if I were alone on that beach, I walked right to the water's edge and knelt down to the wet sand earth, and allowed the waves to wash up against me, gently rising from my knees to my belly.

As if the ocean were a magnet, and the pain within me was its opposite, I imagined the pain draining from my center. Pulling like cords or wires from my center, all different colors of confusion and hurt. They were thick, those cords, but they were going somewhere else besides just coiling and boiling my insides.

I held out my arms, still not aware nor caring who (if anyone) was watching this baptism of sorts, and said, *"There is nothing left of me; I am broken. I do not know how to release this pain. I do not know what I believe in anymore, not in religion, not in love, not in belonging, not in anything. I know the darkest moment of one's life can be the moment of one's greatest rising, but whomever I am talking to here: God? Universe? Spirit? I am going to choose once again to trust in the path. I have no idea where to go from here, but I am here. Bring me home to my breath, please bring me home to myself, and help me start here."*

When I stood up from that kneeling prayer, there was no gold dust that had fallen upon me. There wasn't a symbol from the ocean, like a dolphin's fin cutting through the surface or a stingray swimming by in affirmational approval. There was just me, on a Monday morning, with my work setting toggled to "away" and my mind in the present moment.

The longing to reverse the challenges of my life hadn't subsided. But I was able to just be here—to watch the sun rise and the sun set. The ocean rise, and the ocean fall. The stars appear, and the stars release. It was just me, in human form. Not without pain, not without grief, not without longing for life to be drastically different than it is. And maybe, just being here, feeling the ocean's tide wash up against me, was the bravest thing I could do at that moment. To dare to just be me, unapologetically.

When I returned back to Minnesota, I wish I could say that I took off on a jet plane and all the pain never reached me again. The spell was broken. I became a happily married mother of three in less than four years with triplets; imagine that! I also had a thriving career and published four books in that time. All New York Times Best Sellers, of course. I bought a private island off the coast of Spain, where I started a small goat farm and launched three start-ups with my husband—a three-time Olympic bicyclist and the prince of Egypt. Our babies are gorge, half Egyptian, and half Swedish-German-Norwegian-Irish-and-small-percentages-of-twelve-other-nationalities. They're perfect. And we're just overly, exhaustingly happy all the time. I would then float off on my island, the one with the goats, sipping a daiquiri, while the nanny watches the littles, and I'd smile and say, *everything happens for a reason*.

DOES EVERYTHING HAPPEN FOR A REASON?

I have to say, however, after the next shocking, terrifying, awful event that took place in my life, it made me question that common phrase: *everything happens for a reason*.

While I was writing this book in northern Minnesota, my brother came home. As we all know from reading the pages prior in this book, that as much as TJ wanted to be close to others, he was also an independent. He liked to do things on his own. He was debt-free by thirty, and found a job that paid so much money I told him I'd take *seven years off* of work if I made that in one year and I'd travel the world laughing and blowing snot into my pockets of money. When TJ came home, however, it was because he was not doing well. The pandemic, as many discovered, was extremely harsh on those struggling with anxiety, depression, or loneliness. The pandemic was just *hard* for all of us. I knew that if TJ, the man I had the honor of spending my childhood with and truly felt as if he were a celebrity, was coming home—something must really be wrong.

It was irreversible. He had reached his breaking point, and I thought, *Oh, this is where it gets good, Teej, because this is like the point where it gets really black and dark and sad and lonely and then we spring out of it like we're on a trampoline, remember when I did my first flip on the trampoline? And that one time you dressed up as Spiderman after we watched it in the theatres and told me to pretend like I was in need of desperate help and you'd come and save me somehow, all within the confines of a six-foot trampoline?*

But this time it was different, and what he was fighting was different. The world stopped for my family the summer of 2021. Of course, we still tried to live normal lives like keeping up with work, seeing friends, attending church, but we lived in pulsating panic. *How could this be happening to him?* He asked that himself, while staring into my eyes one terrified night. We banded around my brother like a strong army of warriors standing in the direct line of enemy fire saying *hit me you motherfucker instead of him.* He had had enough mental torture, and we all wished we could just rip it from his existence. But it was his battle and only his battle—and that's just how mental health is—it's not something that can be healed by anyone other than the individual going through it. And even at that, it's infuriatingly challenging to search for the magical concoction that will free this person of their suffering. As with most individuals, TJ didn't want to be on medication. Does anyone want to have to "take something?" There's not only the stigma around taking medication (which, thank God, is becoming more normalized), but there's the list of personal values to wrestle with as well. *Do I need to take medication, or do I just think life should be easier? Am I using this medication as a crutch? Do I actually have a chemical imbalance, or is it circumstantial? Will I become dependent on this? Will I become addicted to it? Is it my genes or a season in my life? Is this something that will go away on its own, or will it always follow me like a dark cloud?*

Just like TJ, I have been extremely leery of taking medication. I've tried a few, namely Lexapro, Zoloft, and Wellbutrin, but across the board, I felt like a zombie and unable to find myself hidden in that numb place of existence. This isn't everyone's experience; some people do great on these medications and they literally save their lives. Everyone's brain chemistry is different. With TJ, there were so many factors, and he wanted to heal himself the natural way. He started meditating to soothe his anxiety around the age of twenty-six. He became a vegetarian (I was really surprised by this, since his diet consisted of Jack's pepperoni and sausage pizzas for four whole years in college), he took hot yoga classes daily for months, he biked and biked and biked as if he were Forrest Gump on a bike. He made goals. He dreamed. He loved. And even him, even TJ, was not exempt from the dreadfully painful problem that is solving a mental illness.

When my sister walked in my room on that Tuesday morning to find me doing yoga, she said, "Mom is here and it's not good news." My heart broke and sank and shook and I already knew. My brother was gone. The illness had done him in, and he was done with his fight. My mother, seated in a chair downstairs, gave me the awful truth—TJ had taken his own life.

In moments such as these, there is a forceful response that happens in the body to such sudden trauma. It pulls your soul from outside of yourself, your body falls in one direction and your soul moves in another. The sound, a loud animalistic scream, lasts as long as it pleases. During it, you wonder, is that me? Like you're watching yourself experience such awful pain and being utterly shocked that it's you. I fell to the floor pressing my face into my hands and my chest into my knees. And then my torso dropped further, between my knees, and they rubbed against the carpeted floor. My hands shook, holding my reddened face with veins of pain pumping from my head to my heart through the softness in my neck. That scream, it just kept coming, consuming all of the oxygen it could find, until there was no more left to give it. It had run out.

And then, there was the ending of my entrance into the camp of grief. Like being uprooted and landed in a heavily forested region where you have no idea where you are, there comes a point where you have to stop crying, get up, look around, and say, *what now?*

They say there are five stages grief, and the first one is Denial. I broke ground for Denial, built a sturdy foundation for Denial, installed the sheetrock of Denial, painted the walls of Denial, hung photos, hauled a kitchen table in with four matching chairs, put brand new hardwood floors in Denial, and really made that place my home. I figured that I may never move from that place, it would be my forever home—just huddled away there in Denial.

The thing about experiencing such trauma is that life still goes on for those living, and they're expected to, you know, brush their teeth, go to meetings for work, eat respectable meals, exercise, pay bills, put new tabs on the car again, and prepare their taxes. My job, as the editor of a lifestyle magazine about happy things including lakeside living, boating, affluent families with mansion homes, and successful artists, became a string pulling me further and further away from my shores of "okayness." I wanted to resurface, and could for a forty-five-minute meeting, but as soon as that meeting was over, I was back in my office releasing more tears and purchasing an embarrassing amount of tissue boxes to replace the ones I was burning through.

The other four stages of grief include Anger, Bargaining, Depression, and Acceptance. These were far-off concepts that I imagined wouldn't find me. I'd just keep hiding from them, staying cozy in Denial. Until I found myself picking up my phone, wanting to just call him and tell him it's not a good idea. *Don't do it, Teej*, I'd say, *we're gonna figure this thing out.* I thought maybe I could send him a message on Facebook? Maybe if I apologized for what I said to him in fifth grade and how I once held up a butcher knife and told him to stop making fun of me and he actually looked scared for the first time in his life of his little sister, then, maybe, he'd come back? Or what if I went to his apartment in Minneapolis again, maybe, would he still be found? Sitting there in his LeBron sweatshirt and black silky sweatpants with the zips on the sides? Maybe he would just be there, waiting for me.

And then there are places one cannot and never should go: What Else Could I Have Done? Why Couldn't I Save Him? These containment camps, found within the heavily forested region of Grief, will starve one completely of their will to keep moving forward in life. It will only build high barricades called Guilt that will keep that individual imprisoned for their entire lives. I had to come to the point, after long dark days and nights of Depression, to the translucent place of Acceptance.

Acceptance isn't an arrival point like when Google Maps tells me in Siri's voice that I've "arrived." It's a place of expansion, like making it out of the heavily forested region just to find yourself in a big old ancient city. And now, you're supposed to figure out how to navigate this big old ancient city with all its triggers, flashing lights, and people walking every which way having not the slightest idea or clue of what you're going through. It's a place one must learn a single street first, something anchoring, like Main Street. Main Street of Acceptance is to walk down memory lane and allow some laughter. Might bust some abdominis muscle fibers over Main Street of memory lane because TJ was hilarious. I would watch videos he sent me, captions he wrote, messages he sent, and just laugh until I cried. A howling cry of a laugh with tears and everything. And then, the next day, after waking to the pang of reality sinking in a little more each day, one ventures down a new street where they'll find Bravery to keep walking and Ceremony to keep their person sacred and Friends to share laughter and Food that reminds you of this person and if one keep going, all the way to the end where the bridge meets the bay, they'll discover Solitude. Solitude is truly the only place where Acceptance can give one its full grace, because it's intimate—this holding of an experience you know that nobody else will ever fully understand. I call it my lock-box of memories: the snapshots of TJ that only I know. Like hidden secrets. Those memories are little rolled up pieces of paper with gold ribbon tied around them and there I keep them, in my lock-box of who TJ was, and always will be, to me.

I didn't know why this had to happen, and I don't believe it's healthy for those who have experienced such gut-wrenching awful things, to ask the heavens above: *why?* Growing up, and all throughout our twenties, it was TJ, my person, whom I was grateful to walk through life with. In my family, with my sisters being much older than us, they were like extra parents. While they are my sisters, and I love them dearly, they weren't the ones who walked with me through kindergarten, middle and high school, and visited me at college. The person he was in my life, that twin-like belonging, isn't something that one can replace nor explain. It's like having a twin and trying to explain to another person what it's like to have a twin. They can only guess at what it actually would be like because they've never experienced it. They don't know the nights playing video games till three in the morning, him making me a "five-star bed" on the floor next to his bed with pillows and blankets so I'd sleep in his room, or the way he'd stare in awe at me as I made life-quaking choices, or the father-like voice he'd use on the phone with me when I told him about my near-misses and injurious experiences, or the way he always wanted to sit next to me at the dinner table so he could make fun of my messy eating. There just wouldn't be another him.

How does one cope with such a reality? I am not sure anyone can correctly explain how they keep moving forward, besides just a single moment at a time. And allowing their person's spirit to show up at times. It is my belief that, if we ask, their spirit will show us something: a song, a signal, a bird, a rain or wind, and that is a little wink showing you that their spirit is still here.

The next day, after my brother's passing, I sat outside on my sister's patio next to a pond with aged evergreen trees all around it standing calmly. I said, out loud, just like I always must do when I'm speaking to God or Universe, *I cannot live without you, TJ, you know that, so I need you to show me somehow that you're still with me.*

Just as I finished that heavy prayer, a swirl of wind came rushing from across the pond, making the trees sway in obedience to this strong force. It swirled and swirled, like the trees were dancing in a circle, an audible whip. It moved across the pond, rippling the water, and pulling the molecules up making dimples across the smooth surface. The wind kept circling until it washed right over me, encompassing all of me, soothing my tear-stained cheeks, and making the curls around my face dance and brush beside my temples. I sat high and proud. I smiled a painful smile, held my hands out, and then spoke to him like I would normally speak to him. As real as it gets: *okay—then you're not getting out of this goddamnit, you're coming with me through every circumstance in life. When I need to vent, ya gonna hear it. When I need to cry, ya gonna know it. When I need a friend, you better be there holding me and telling me it will all be okay. You're not going anywhere; you're staying right here with me.*

The next five months after June of 2021, went just like the days following my accident from the tree—in a spiritual fog. I do not recall even caring for myself such as eating or the process of being awake to fall asleep again, but I was, and I kept on somehow moving forward. I got dressed and went to work. I ached and tried to hide my tears until I no longer felt the need to hide my tears. I thought of Native American tribes and began researching how they grieve the loss of their loved ones. Many Native tribes believe that their loved ones do not die, they "walk on." They release the spirit onward through loud drumming, dancing, howling, singing, wailing, and even cut their hair to display a period of mourning. It's a celebratory send-off. I craved something like that, but in America, we have emails on Monday that need responses and deadlines quickly approaching. In America, we are expected to package our grief, like one of those vacuum bags for storage, just suck all the air out and store it somewhere—then don't open it for a really, really long time. When it finally gets opened again, all the air comes rushing in, life breathes back into the bag, and there the contents sit, just the same as when they were suctioned away.

I needed a way, like a Native American pounding, to release this thing. To feel the sensations on my skin, to sweat, to yell in anger and frustration and longing. So, I started boxing. In November of that year, I stood on a straight line with five other women, hands wrapped, gloves tightly bound, and bowed in to my first boxing class. On a padded mat, we warmed up by running in a wide circle listening to soundtracks by Rob Zombie, Disturbed, Slipknot, and Shinedown. Not typical music I'd listen to, but there was something in this music, *hello darkness my old friend*, that I found relatable. I was living in *restless dreams, I walked alone*. Because as much as your living loved ones want to support you, they have no clue what it's like to be you. They have no idea the depth of the hurt or the isolation of the grievous cry that sectioned you forever to a new camp of life. But there is one thing that ties all of humanity together, and that is the fact that pain is pain. Whether it's a child who passed at birth, a mother who passed from cancer, a spouse who passed from a car accident, a sister who went missing and was never found, the slow death of divorce and the splitting apart of a once happy home—there is this big, wide, cavernous well of pain where all of these people, like everyone in the entire world, places their tears.

Though they come from different sources, and from different people, pain is pain. And that's how we can heal one another, is just to be seen. I believe that is all anyone ever desires in this life, is just to be seen for who they are. It is my hope, as this book is quickly coming to a close, to offer a prayer to anyone who will ever read this book and is feeling alone—to think back to that deep well that is all of the world's pain and trauma placed right there in the open for everyone to see. No more hiding. And if this individual, this sweet human life, has the bravery to take their pain and show it to all the others standing at that well, this "wailing well" of sorts, they may discover that their situation is unique to them, but their pain, that awful pulsating place deep, deep within them they so desperately wish to rip from themselves, is shared by all of humanity at some point in their lives.

These boxing ladies and the fact that *I needed to be somewhere* held me up like a strong tower. I'd be at work, beginning to cry, and start listening to Slipknot and writing on my calendar BOXING in all caps and then sit there and draw a rectangle around it over and over again. The class lasted an hour, but if I could've, I would've stayed for three or four, facing my partner and practicing jab-jab-cross, cross-upper-hook, right kick, left kick, right kick, three knees and sprawl. Hit and hit and hit, harder and harder, until I felt I had actually broken my wrist or fractured my foot. I looked like a severely abused woman walking around with bruises everywhere until I noticed that even my body got used to that, it adjusted to the intense impact whacking my knees as I rammed them into pads over and over again. Our bodies adjust, just as our lives, somehow, someway, eventually adjust too.

Perhaps there is an unscathed human out there, living in perfect condition. If I were an item being sold on Facebook Marketplace right now, I'd have to say I'm neither "new" or "like-new," not even "good" or "fairly used," I am the last category they forgot to add, "beaten, broken, probably with severe emotional trauma, but damnit she still works and wow when she does it's like the stars conspire, sparkle, crinkle, and it's a beautifully broken masterpiece." The irony in this story, is that I am completing it at the age of twenty-nine, that *peachy-free* age of twenty-nine where Prince Charming was meant to arrive and we'd waltz off into the sunset like giddy slap-happy lovers and pain, what's pain? It would cease to exist.

Twenty-nine didn't arrive with that effortless freedom that I thought it would bring when I was twenty-six. Someone else did not arrive in my life and say *here, give me all that's hurting you so I can just take it and will love you unconditionally.* That's an act that can only be performed a force much greater than us, an all-knowing, overflowing with love, God or Spirit or Universe or Creator or whatever you've chosen to use here. What twenty-nine did bring, in its absence, is what I can only describe as the unbreakable belief in myself that no matter how life turns for the worst and what was once the best thing gets broken into a million tiny little pieces on the hardwood floor in front of me, I can and will find a way to move forward. In truth, I'd rather take the pain, confusion, trauma, and brokenness because in all of those things comes the true discovery of one's core. There is a place, within every single human being, where pure peace exists. For me, it was not holding onto the ideals that haunted me and forced me into plastic cutouts of a life that I thought I was meant to live. I get to be the pottery. That damp piece of earthen clay, being shaped and molded, spun and then broken, added to, taken away, and finally built precisely how it was meant to be—an image of how God always wanted me.

This place of peace, accessible to every being at its most authentic core, only asks one thing: *to let it be*. Let the pain come and wash in like great waves, let life crack you open, allow what was said all those years ago to hurt you, what was done to you, what didn't go as it should have, the poor hand of cards you were dealt, the times you failed, the times others were disappointed in you, the times you were disappointed in yourself, the times you wish so desperately to erase from history—they're all there to build the strongest, most compassionate, loving, giving, warrior of a human you'll ever have the chance to meet.

Because the opposite of *let it be* is to *force it away*. Forcing anything in life will never bring the results we desire, so, instead, we get the opportunity to let it sit there until our own inner garden of peace becomes so overflowingly expansive that it ceases to control us any longer. In the year following my brother's passing, I decided to keep growing my inner garden through daily meditation and the repetitive practice of yoga. To keep releasing the hurt I held in my chest like tiny droplets of water. It was both a reminder of the love I kept, my lock-box of memories, and understanding that the spiritual realm existed long before me and will exist long after. Even when I feel alone, I remember the wailing well, where all of humanity holds its pain, and that it too can hold mine. It is both sides, the joy and the hurt of life, that makes us beautifully, individually, and collectively human.

And with it, I made one pact with myself for thirty: *to let it be, proudly and imperfectly.*

*** The End ***

ACKNOWLEDGMENTS

To my mother, Jayne, and my father, Gregg, who gave me all the tools to remove anything from myself that was not authentic to me. To my sisters, Mandi and Anna, for being strong towers. To my brother, TJ, for being my protector, best friend, and spirit. To my friends who have supported me since middle school, you are irreplaceable. To anyone feeling alone right now, I hope you give life another chance. To my editor, Adrienne Jongquist, for speaking your truth and helping me clarify mine. To my publishers, Chip and Jean Borkenhagen with RiverPlace Press, for their years of experience and unwavering belief in me as a developing author. To the Five Wings Art Council (fwac.org) for seeing potential in this project and funding the means to complete it. To anyone working on a new project, keep going. To anyone walking through grief, keep going. To anyone discouraged by failure, keep going. To anyone reading this, just keep going.

ABOUT THE AUTHOR

Emilee Mae is a native of northcentral Minnesota and a graduate of Minnesota State University, Mankato, with a degree in creative writing. She has published works in *Sun Valley Magazine, Boise Territory, Western Home Journal, South 85 Journal, Storyville Projects I* and *II, Lake Country Journal*, and Merrell.com, where she participated as a sponsored outdoor athlete. She resides in northwest Florida and works as an editor and practitioner of the healing arts.

Contact information:
Website: emileemae.com
Twitter: @writerlyfe
Instagram: @emileemaewrites
Facebook: @emileemaeauthor